A hilarious account of spiritual globetrotting, *Jesus without Borders* is an insightful travelogue on how local culture shapes Christian culture around the world.

—JONATHAN MERRITT, author, *Jesus Is Better Than You Imagined*; senior columnist, Religion News Service

I love how Chad Gibbs sees the world and God, and how he translates that onto these pages for the rest of us to learn from, laugh at, and genuinely enjoy. I'm grateful for his words and for his journey and for this book.

—ANNIE F. DOWNS, author, *Let's All Be Brave*

Faith is not just what we believe. It's a product of our environment and upbringing and a hundred other factors. And maybe, as Chad shares in this book, that's not such a bad thing. A faith that isn't affected by where you are and who you're with is just dead orthodoxy; *Jesus without Borders* gives you something much more vibrant to hold onto. I loved the writing and the message in this book.

—JEFF GOINS, author, *The Art of Work*

Using humor, insight, and a well-stamped passport, Gibbs explores the lenses through which we look at our faith, and sparks our imagination to wonder what we might discover if we had the courage to look beyond our cultural biases and see Jesus with new eyes.

—SARAH THEBARGE, author, *The Invisible Girls*

JESUS WITHOUT BORDERS

JESUS WITHOUT BORDERS

WHAT PLANES, TRAINS, AND RICKSHAWS TAUGHT ME ABOUT JESUS

CHAD GIBBS

ZONDERVAN

Jesus without Borders

This title is also available as a Zondervan ebook.
Visit www.zondervan.com/ebooks.

This title is not available on papyrus scroll.

Requests for information should be addressed to:
Zondervan, *3900 Sparks Dr. SE, Grand Rapids, Michigan 49546*

ISBN: 978-0-310-32554-3

Author's note: Some of the names in this book have been changed. Not legally, mind you; I don't have that sort of authority. The names have been changed only in the pages of this book, and this was done by request, not because I thought the person's parents did a poor job naming them.

Cover design: Jarrod Taylor
Interior photography: Chad Gibbs
Interior design: Mark Sheeres

First printing January 2015/Printed in the United States of America

As always,
for Tricia

CONTENTS

PROLOGUE

"This is an interesting planet. It deserves all the attention you can give it."

—Marilynne Robinson, *Gilead*

When I was seven, I asked Santa Claus for the USS *Flagg*, a *Nimitz*-class aircraft carrier used by the real American heroes of G.I. Joe in their fight against Cobra. At seven and a half feet long, this was perhaps the largest toy ever manufactured, and throughout the fall, I spent hours staring at photographs of it in the Sears Wish Book. Santa, however, in his infinite wisdom, realized my room wasn't big enough to hold the USS *Flagg* and my bed at the same time. Santa also made the logical assumption that my parents, like most adults, did not want to spend the next three years with an aircraft carrier for a coffee table. So on Christmas morning, I received a bunch of size-appropriate toys and a light-up globe.

The globe was not my favorite gift that morning. In fact it was my least favorite gift that wasn't socks. Globes, as you may know, don't do a whole lot. I remember spinning it a few times, finding a country named Chad, then briefly considering painting it gray and pretending it was the Death Star, but the scale was all off. So instead I just set it on my nightstand and wondered how good a kid would have to be before Santa brought him a USS *Flagg*.

I don't recall exactly when the tradition began, but soon after Christmas, and every night for a long time, my sister and I would turn off the lights, switch on the globe, and spin the glowing orb, stopping it seconds later with our finger on the spot where we would live when we grew up.

"I'm going to live in Saudi Arabia."

"I'm going to live in Chile."

"I'm going to live in Greenland."

"I'm going to live adrift in the Atlantic Ocean."

Water has always been a problem for globe-spinning expatriate predictions, since it covers about 70 percent of the earth's surface, but we never cared, because it gave us another chance to spin what eventually became my favorite gift of Christmas 1985.

I didn't read a lot of books as a kid, but I spent hours flipping through our ten-year-old set of *World Book Encyclopedia*.[1] I'd read about all sorts of things like dinosaurs and the Teapot Dome Scandal, but mostly I'd read about the countries my globe prophesied I'd live in one day. Places with the tallest mountains and bluest lakes and driest deserts I'd ever seen. It all looked so different from Glencoe, Alabama, but it all felt so close, because my globe made the world feel smaller. Of course I'll see Poland one day. Why wouldn't I visit Mongolia? Never mind that my parents had never left the country and I'd never been farther from home than Panama City Beach, Florida. I was going to see the world. I knew it.

■ ■ ■

Let the record show that globes are terrible prognosticators. When I married Tricia in 2005, I was twenty-seven years old and had lived my entire life in Alabama. I'd never been to Poland. I'd never seen Mongolia. I'd never left the country, and not only that, I'd never even left the South.

Our honeymoon changed this, but not drastically. We flew from Birmingham to the Bahamas, an island chain you can spit on from

1. If you were born too late to know what the *World Book Encyclopedia* is, just imagine fitting all of Wikipedia in your parents' hall closet.

Miami if the wind is favorable. At that time, you didn't even need a passport to visit the Bahamas, just a copy of your birth certificate and a smile. We spent all of our time there in an all-inclusive luxury resort, though from what I gathered on the high-speed van ride from the airport, luxury is not a word associated with everyday Bahamian life. But in our defense, this was our honeymoon. We didn't exactly go there to soak up local culture.

I was thirty-one before I finally left the South. Tricia had a week off during her medical residency and I planned a whirlwind trip that took us to Washington, D.C., New York City, and Boston, all by car, because over the years I'd built up a healthy fear of air travel, a fear our bumpy honeymoon flight had done nothing to alleviate.

Fear had played a major role in my lack of travel through the years. With work, I had opportunities to fly to conferences in exotic places like Des Moines or Milwaukee, but I always declined because there were people out there who hijacked airplanes and crashed them into buildings. And I certainly didn't want to leave America, because those people who hate America live outside of America, and they would be waiting on me. Home was familiar and safe, and I was happy never to leave it.

But it was that trip to the Northeast that rekindled my desire to see the world, a desire born of nightly adolescent globe spinning. As a kid, there was nothing scary about the idea of traveling to a place like New York City. All I had to do was jump in a car or hop on a plane or climb on my bike, and then I could actually see the Empire State Building and the Statue of Liberty and all those other things I read about in the N-O volume of our encyclopedia. Somewhere along the way I lost that adventurous disposition, but standing there in Central Park, I found it again. Travel was possible, and it was fun. I was a kid again.

"Are we really here?" I asked Tricia.

"Yes, we are."

"You know, we haven't spent my first book advance from Zondervan. Let's go to Europe next summer."

"Okay, let's do it!"

■ ■ ■

My next travel conversation with Tricia wasn't quite so adventurous. Well, it was adventurous, but only in an afraid-to-fly sort of way, because after a quick look at the map, I was reminded that Europe is not easily accessible from the United States by car.

"Even if there is a ferry service across the Bering Strait," Tricia said, "we are not taking it."

"Why not?"

"Because we are not driving through Russia to get to Italy."

"Why not?"

"Because we—because *I* am not insane."

"Well, what about the *Queen Mary 2*?" I asked.

"What about it?"

"We could drive to New York again, then sail across the Atlantic. It takes only seven days, and I read it has a great breakfast buffet."

"Sure, and spend two of our three weeks on a boat. We are flying, or we are not going."

She was right, of course. There is only one practical way to get from Alabama to Europe, and that is to sit inside a 132-ton aluminum tube while it hurtles thirty-seven thousand feet over the Atlantic Ocean at 531 mph. So that's how we went, and in the end I suppose eight hours in a plane beats a sixteen-day drive across Siberia, though the latter would make an excellent reality show.

The Euro trip was supposed to scratch our travel itch for many years to come, but instead it left me itching all over.[2] We went to Rome, Florence, Venice, Paris, and London, and when we landed in Atlanta three weeks later, I was already reading departure signs, wondering where we could go next. Not that it was a perfect vacation. On our third day, I fell off a metro platform in Rome and thought I was going to be ripped in two. And later, on our overnight train to Paris, some creepy dude broke into our room in a pathetic attempt to rob us, turning and

2. Not literally, though the bedbugs in some European hotels might require a trip to the dermatologist for some ointment.

running away when he noticed we were awake and staring at him from our bunk beds. Tricia even got tired of being around me twenty-four hours a day and became more annoyed that I didn't seem tired of being around her so much. No, there were good days and bad days, but I realized that I truly love to travel.

I love the planning, the packing, the waiting in airports, and even the airplane food. I love wandering jet-lagged through some foreign city because the hotel won't let you check in until 2:00 p.m. I love going somewhere cold when it's hot at home, and going somewhere hot when it's cold. I love getting lost and asking for directions in a language I don't speak. I love calling my bank to alert them of my travel plans, and I love finding strange currency in my pockets months after a trip. I love buying travel guides and applying for visas and even getting vaccines, because that usually means I'm going somewhere really interesting. I love it all, and since it took me more than thirty years to find this passion, I wanted to make up for lost time.

■ ■ ■

On our excellent adventure, Tricia and I attended a handful of church services in some of Europe's grandest cathedrals. This was not because we are so pious that we never miss a Sunday but because tours of these grand cathedrals cost money, while attending, say, a Tuesday prayer service is free.

Worshiping God in a foreign country reminded me of my childhood trips to Panama City Beach. I realize that previous sentence is perhaps counterintuitive, but hear me out. When I was a kid, we never went to church on vacation. At the beach, Sundays were spent building sandcastles, same as Tuesdays or Fridays. But we'd drive past churches on our way to eat seafood or play putt-putt golf, and I remember it was a revelation to me that people actually go to church here, that Christianity even exists in this place that felt so different from home.

I believe self-centered is the human default setting. Oftentimes we think about others only when we are wondering what they are thinking about us. As we grow older, we think of our lives as movies, and when we're not in a scene, the action stops. But here's the thing: I'm almost positive that when I am not in Panama City Beach, life is still going on there. Men and women are going to work, kids are going to school, tourists are shopping at Alvin's Island, and believers are worshiping God.

As a kid I knew life was different outside of Glencoe. I knew it was different because I'd read about it, and I dreamed about seeing it one day. But as I grew older, life became routine, and when life becomes routine, we forget about everything but the routine. And sure, on some level we still know life is different "out there," but as little as we consider it, we might as well not know it at all.

I was thirty-two years old before I realized there is more to life than Auburn football and vacations at the beach, and this scared me. What if living my entire life in the buckle of the Bible Belt had given me not only a narrow view of the world but also a narrow view of my faith? What if the culture I'd grown up in, the deep-fried, sweet-tea, biscuits-and-gravy culture of the Deep South, was in some ways hindering my relationship with Christ? It's the only culture I've experienced, so if it was hindering my faith, how would I even know?

Because local culture has to play a large role in shaping local Christian culture, right? Take the South, for example. I've lived my entire life in a deeply conservative, fiercely patriotic part of the country. A culture of honor, where men are quick to throw a punch, but just as quick to go out of their way to help a stranger. A place where racism has been a bit of a problem, to put it mildly. Consequently I've sung "red and yellow, black and white, they are precious in his sight" in a church that has never had a black member. And I've pledged my allegiance to the flag of the United States of America in the same worship service where I've sung "this world is not my home."

My faith has been shaped by my culture, and yours has too, and so were Peter's and Paul's, and I think that's okay, because how could they not be? But not all parts of our cultures are compatible with the life Christ has called us to live, and when our culture is all we know, this isn't easy to see. I wanted to see the world because I love to travel, but more than that, I wanted to experience Christian culture around the world because I believed doing so could change me for the better. I believed that seeing the work of Christ across the globe could only deepen my relationship with him and that conversing with fellow believers from cultures vastly different from my own would perhaps shed some light on any cultural biases that were hindering my faith. And I wanted to write about my experiences because I hoped the things I learned could help you too, while providing me with some excellent tax deductions.

St. Augustine said, "The world is a book and those who do not travel read only one page."[3] It was time I turned the page.

■ ■ ■

I assumed there was a book like this one out there already. The general market is flooded with travel books, and nowadays one is almost always sitting on my nightstand, where my globe used to be. But the Christian market is almost devoid of travel books, unless you count books about children who travel to heaven and back, in which case there is a surprising abundance. There are books about and by missionaries too, but that's not exactly what I'm writing about here, though I do think traveling can lead to a more missional life. I wanted to travel because God is at work all around the world, and I wanted to see it.

I believed in this book before I ever took the first trip. I was convinced that traveling the world and experiencing Christian cultures different from my own would transform my worldview, deepen my relationship with Christ, and perhaps even alter the trajectory of my life for years to come. I was convinced. However, there was still one other person who needed convincing.

■ ■ ■

"You want to visit how many countries?"

"Twelve," I said, then named them while Tricia let out a long sigh.

---

3. Or maybe he didn't say this, because after a few hours of searching, I couldn't find the source of this quote. But around 8.6 million websites attribute the quote to Augustine, so he might as well have said it.

"Why stop at twelve?" she said. "Why not visit all 196 countries in the world?"

I began to explain that I believed the twelve I'd picked were a good representation of the world at large, but then realized Tricia was being facetious, so I stopped talking.

"And how exactly do you propose we pay for these twelve international trips?" Tricia asked.

I knew this question was coming, and I was ready for it because I'd recently discovered travel hacking, a somewhat bizarre method of earning boatloads of frequent flier miles. If I could pay for my flights with frequent flier miles, and if I could pay for a friend's flight with frequent flier miles, and if that friend would split hotel costs with me, I theorized I could write this book for around fifteen thousand dollars, which, incidentally, is about how much I expected my advance to be if a publisher picked up the book.[4]

"Do you really think you can find someone to go with you to each of these countries?" Tricia asked, after rolling her eyes at my frequent flier miles scheme.

"Of course. It's a free flight. Who wouldn't want to go?"

We sat in silence for a moment while I shuffled through the spreadsheets I'd created detailing how affordable the trips could actually be, then Tricia finally said, "Okay, tell me why you want to write this book again?"

So I began telling her how I wanted to see the work of Christ across the globe because I believed doing so could deepen my faith, but as I spoke, my mind drifted to all the soccer matches I'd be able to see in each country. And then I started to see holes in the book, one being that I'm not the most adventurous eater, and travel books usually involve some degree of adventurous eating. I wondered if people would grow tired of reading about the differences between McNuggets in Hong Kong and McNuggets in Moscow. Then an even bigger issue with the book raised its head—namely that I would spend only about one

---

4. In the end I was only about a thousand off. If you're interested in the details, check out the appendix: "A Call to Travel."

week in each country, and in seven days I'd experience only a sliver of Christian culture in each place. But it's not like I could spend a year in each country, and even if I could, I'm not sure that would be enough time either. In the end I could only catch glimpses, but sometimes a glimpse is all you need.

I finished explaining the book and Tricia thought for a long moment before finally saying, "If we can really pay for the flights with frequent flier miles, and if, and only if, someone agrees to publish it, you can go around the world."

I was shocked at how quickly Tricia agreed to let me take this crazy adventure. Permission to drive around the South and write about college football is one thing; permission to fly around the world is something else entirely.

"Okay," I said, then pressed my luck a little. "Why don't we take one trip so I can write a sample chapter, then I'll pitch the idea to publishers, and if one of them wants the book, I'll take the rest of the trips?"

"And if no one wants the book?"

"If no one wants the book, I'll cash out my frequent flier miles and buy a USS *Flagg*." Tricia didn't smile, so I added, "If no one wants the book, we'll just call this trip a vacation and I'll find something else to write about."

"That sounds good," she said.

"Alright, well, where do you want to go?"

"When my sister and I were little, we had a globe, and we'd spin it every night and say where we were going to live when we were older. Since then I've always wanted to see Brazil."

I couldn't help but smile. "Pack your bags," I said. "We're going to Brazil."

■ ■ ■

And we went to Brazil, and then I went to a whole list of countries that before had only been names on a globe, and what follows is what happened as best as I can remember. But before you turn the page, I want to remind you that travel writer Paul Theroux said, "Travel is glamorous only in retrospect," and truer words may have never been spoken. To write this book, I spent more than two weeks of my life on airplanes, and another week just sitting inside airports. There were frustrations. Flights were delayed. I got lost. I got sick. I got a greater appreciation for Western toilets. I remember lying on a bench in Tokyo Narita Airport with a throbbing migraine wondering how they'd get my body home if my head exploded. At times I missed Tricia and our son, Linus, so much I became physically ill. But there is something magical about travel. In the weeks after you come home, the bad parts of a trip fade into the dark corners of your mind, leaving only the sunny days and delicious meals and happy times with new friends. All this is to say that travel is never perfect, but this project was the experience of a lifetime, and I wouldn't change a single moment of it. Well, maybe one moment in a Russian Orthodox church, but we'll get to that in a bit.

BRAZIL

When twilight dims the sky above,
recalling thrills of our love,
there's one thing I'm certain of:
Return, I will, to old Brazil.

—Ary Barroso, "Brazil"

Mr. Gibbs, what was the reason for your visit to Brazil?"

The immigration officer stood waiting for an answer to the question I'd been dreading since we arrived back on American soil a little before four in the morning. I wasn't dreading the question in a "so I could stuff my body cavities with contraband and sneak it into the country" sort of way; it was just that, to be honest, I didn't have any reason for visiting Brazil. The trip was the result of a surplus of frequent flier miles, an idea for a book that no publisher had agreed to publish, and my wife's having a couple of days off work in early November. However, none of those things sounded like a reasonable explanation to give that frowning person who, I believed, had the authority to send me straight to Guantanamo Bay.

Preceding this trip, my knowledge of Brazil was sketchy at best. I knew where it is on the globe, because, as you know, I once owned a globe. I also knew Brazil is the world's leading exporter of swimsuit models. But apart from these things, when I thought of Brazil, I wasn't really sure what to think. Which is why Tricia and I spent most of our flight frantically reading about Brazil in the various travel guides we'd borrowed from the Auburn Public Library, which was probably unaware we planned to take the guides out of the country.

Tricia was the first to find a fun fact. "Did you know that if you don't include Alaska, Brazil is actually larger than the United States?"

"Why wouldn't we include Alaska?"

"I don't know. That's just what the book says."

"If we count only states called Rhode Island, Switzerland is larger than the United States. Your book is stupid."

"You're stupid, Geography Boy."

We touched down a little before 10:00 a.m. at Galeao International Airport and made our way through customs, which in Brazil is efficient, though perhaps less than thorough.

"Are you bringing things into our country you shouldn't?"

"No."

"Good! Welcome to Brazil."

Most everything in the arrivals terminal was written in Portuguese, but an official sign told us in English that the airport advised using the prepaid taxi services, which were being run by hysterical women in booths who kept screaming, "You want taxi!" at every person who walked past them. We figured such an official sign couldn't be wrong, so we approached one of these women, and once she calmed down, we gave her R$99 for safe passage to our hotel.

The tropical spring air of Brazil was quite a contrast with the late autumn day we'd left behind in Atlanta, but before I could even comment, a man with a walkie-talkie grabbed my receipt and began pointing and yelling at several other men equally armed with walkie-talkies. I feared they were discussing which ones would hold us down while the others stole our money, but soon we found ourselves in the back of an unmarked black cab with a driver who, apparently, mistook us for Hollywood stunt drivers looking to be impressed.

Once on the Avenida Brasil (a street name that I believe translates as "Avenue of Fiery Death"), I realized our driver was just driving the way it seemed all Brazilians drive, like inebriated Earnhardts. There was lots of swerving and accelerating, but then we hit traffic and it was a slow trudge, except for the motorcycles, which zipped down the highway between lanes of traffic, constantly honking their horns, lest someone open a door and ruin their day. At places where the traffic had stopped completely, men, women, and children were out walking among the cars, selling sodas and snacks while dodging motorcycles. I thought vehicle-to-vehicle salesman has to be one of the five worst jobs on the planet.

Driving from the airport through Rio's North Zone, we passed many poor neighborhoods. Tricia and I exchanged "what have we gotten ourselves into" looks as we drove by abandoned buildings, run-down housing projects, and of course Brazil's famed favelas.

The favelas are beautiful from a distance. Multicolored buildings running up mountainsides give you the impression you're looking at a Mediterranean vacation village. But on closer inspection, you realize these villas are actually shacks, home to Brazil's poor. Drug lords and other deviants are scattered throughout the favelas, though it would be wrong to assume everyone living there would enjoy robbing you at gunpoint—a hyperbolic assertion I came across on a message board or two. That being said, the favelas do have some pretty astronomical murder rates, which is why Tricia and I had no plans to visit them on our trip.

We arrived, by the grace of God, a little after noon at our hotel, where we splashed some water in our eyes before walking down to Copacabana Beach, perhaps the most famous beach in the world.

Copacabana Beach is almost two and a half miles long and shaped like a crescent moon, and the first thing you notice is how wide it is. This is because the hotels are all across Avenida Atlantica, leaving the sand unspoiled for volleyball nets, soccer goals, and workout equipment.

As for beach attire, what you and I call skimpy, Brazilians call modest. Men, women, and children all were in Speedos and G-strings, and none seemed the least bit self-conscious about it. And sure, some of them had the bodies to pull off these swimsuits, or lack thereof, but many did not. Still, no one seemed to care. "Surprisingly," Tricia said, "this place does wonders for your body image." And I guess it does. Go to Copacabana Beach and you won't be the best looking person in a skimpy swimsuit, but you certainly won't be the worst.

We dipped our feet in the Atlantic, which was freezing, then took a stroll up the beach, dodging frisbees and soccer balls, quickly turning our heads when we saw more of someone's behind than we wanted to see. After a while we walked back up toward the road and walked a little more on the Portuguese pavement of the Copacabana promenade, stopping later for a burger at one of the beachside cafes.

"Are we really here?" Tricia asked, staring down the beach at the waves crashing into Morro do Leme.

"Well, if it's a dream, let's not pay for lunch."

But it wasn't a dream. We were in Brazil, looking out at the most spectacular stretch of ocean I'd ever seen, eating average hamburgers and struggling to stay awake. Anything seemed possible.

■ ■ ■

That evening Creedence Clearwater Revival asked through our taxi's speakers if we'd ever seen the rain. It was early Friday evening now, and we were on our way to church. I don't get the impression that Brazilians typically attend church on Friday night; they seem to be Sunday morning folks, like us. But this was a new church, and they were trying new things. In fact this was the first ever service for this church, which was going to be called River Church.[1]

In the weeks leading up to this trip, I'd scoured the internet searching for churches to visit and believers to talk to, and when I came across River Church, I couldn't believe my eyes. Not because a church was holding its first service the day we would arrive, which was quite a coincidence, but because Andrew, the man starting it, is from Sylacauga, Alabama, about an hour's drive from where we live.

I contacted Andrew immediately to find out why someone from the 'Cauga was starting a church in Rio de Janeiro. Turns out Andrew had married a Brazilian, Juliana, and the two of them had spent time in Europe and Africa and were now back in Rio to start a church.

Tonight was the first of three "prelaunch" services for River Church, and Andrew planned to lay out the mission of the new church to the forty or so folks who would show up. We were, I suspect, the only international visitors.

River Church had rented an auditorium on the second floor of Centro Empresarial Botafogo, a high-rise building in Rio, and upstairs we met Andrew, who gave the impression of a man who'd spent the previous ten hours pounding double espressos. I'd never given much thought to starting a church, but apparently there are a lot of moving parts, and Andrew was in charge of most of them. Tonight the video screen was not cooperating, and Andrew was anxiously trying to get it working. Even so, he stopped to greet us, thanking us repeatedly for the two large jars of creamy peanut butter, a delicacy hard to come by in Brazil, that we'd ~~smuggled~~ brought from the States. Then he asked, "Will you two stand here and greet people as they arrive?"

---

1. Rio de Janeiro actually means "January River." The Portuguese explorers who discovered it on January 1, 1502, thought they'd found the mouth of a mighty river. They had not.

Tricia said yes before I could say no, and we took our posts at the door.

"You do realize we don't speak Portuguese?"

"So?"

"So, welcoming them in English might not be very welcoming."

We'd looked over some common Portuguese phrases on the plane and tried to remember what the word for welcome is, but neither of us could. It was like a test we'd forgotten to study for. Soon the first visitors to River Church were arriving, and we decided to just smile and nod as they passed through.

After the first group, I told Tricia the smiling and nodding was a little creepy. "They probably think we're brainwashed and they're joining a cult." Just then Andrew came running by and I asked for the Portuguese word for welcome.

"Boas-vindas," he said.

"Boas-vindas," we repeated.

And when the next group came through, we greeted them with a hearty "boas-vindas," to which they replied, in perfect English, "Thanks. Are you two from the States?"

The service was supposed to begin at 7:00 p.m., but now it was 7:30, and Andrew explained that River Church would be run on Rio time, which meant it was after 9:00 p.m. before a couple of guys took the stage and began to play worship songs. The tunes were familiar Chris Tomlin, Hillsong, and Jesus Culture songs, but the words were very Portuguese. The good thing about worship songs, though, is you tend to repeat six words over and over for the better part of half an hour, so we soon found ourselves praising God in a foreign language,[2] which was pretty cool. From time to time the singer switched to English, which was great, but by the end I kind of preferred the Portuguese.

After thirty minutes of worship, Andrew and Maria, one of the founding members of River Church, took the stage to talk about the church's mission. At first Andrew spoke in English, while Maria

---

2. I'm assuming that's what we were doing, though I can't rule out the possibility that the whole time we were singing about mayonnaise.

translated into Portuguese, then after a few sentences, they switched languages. It was impressive, and I began to wonder if linguistic gymnastics had been added to the 2016 Olympic Games in Rio and these two were training for the gold.

"We are a relationship movement," Andrew said, "unified, not defined by what divides us, but defined by the power and presence of God, on us and through us."

The passion in Andrew's voice was evident, and I scanned the room of attentive faces, wishing we could move here to be a part of this new church. This new adventure.

"Our assignment is simple," Andrew said in closing, "transform the planet."

And with that, some people went down front and prayed for the future of the new church, while Tricia and I made our way toward the food in the back.[3] While I was stuffing my face with little ham sandwiches, Tricia began talking to Claudia, a young woman we'd met earlier in the lobby.

Turns out Claudia had spent the last two years studying in the States, first at the University of Wisconsin in Madison, where she earned her PhD, then at Johns Hopkins in Baltimore for her postdoctoral fellowship. When I'm intimidated by someone's intelligence, as I was with Claudia's, I tend to ask dumber questions than normal. "So why do you guys paint lines on your roads if no one pays attention to them anyway?" Claudia smiled at me the way I smile at my nephew when he tells the world his diaper is stinky, then she turned around and resumed smart person talk with Tricia.

We hung around fellowshiping for an hour or so, but it was getting late, and despite the Brazilian coffee River Church was serving, Tricia and I were exhausted from our thirty-six-hour day. We said goodnight to Andrew, Juliana, and the rest of the wonderful people we'd met and then took a taxi back to the hotel for a night of dreamless sleep.

■ ■ ■

3. Shut up, we were starving.

The River Church service felt similar to a typical service back home in so many ways, but still there were obviously some differences between believers here and believers back home; I was just having trouble putting my finger on them.[4] After we returned home, I spoke to Emilio, a friend of a friend, and a Brazilian pastor of a Presbyterian church in Brasilia. "Protestants are the minority here," he told me, "unlike in the USA, and for decades there was some persecution of Protestants—not too harsh, but still. Back then, people who claimed to be Protestants really meant it, but more recently this group has grown to the point that you now have many nominal Protestants, like you do in the States and like many Catholics here."

Emilio attended seminary in Mississippi, so I was eager to ask him what differences he saw between Christians in the US and Christians in Brazil. His answer surprised me.

"Christians in Brazil tend to be way less involved in politics. We are not a society that has two parties with clear stances like the US does. Things here are much more nuanced, and voting for a given party relates very little to your religious affiliation. I see American Christians naively associating their country with the kingdom of God; here believers are less prone to such things. We are less enthusiastic about our country's history, military achievements, anthem singing,[5] and all of that. It's not a lack of patriotism; it's just a greater separation between a citizenship in heaven and one on earth. There would never be a flag ceremony or singing of the national anthem during a church service here."

Living in Alabama my entire life, I've gone to my share of God and country services at church, and for years I never thought twice about American flags in the sanctuary or wondered why "The Star-Spangled Banner" is in the Baptist hymnal or even considered how "God Bless America" must sound to foreign ears. But lately I've been more concerned with these things, not because I'm unpatriotic or because I'm

4. The differences, not the believers.

5. I assume now that Emilio was talking about anthem singing in church, because anyone who watched the 2014 World Cup knows that Brazilians are really into anthem singing.

ungrateful for the sacrifices that have been made by our servicemen and women, but because I'm not sure why we so eagerly want to associate our imperfect country with a perfect God. I've read the Bible, and unless I missed it while skimming through parts of Numbers, the United States of America isn't mentioned. Yet so many of us have a hard time believing God would have a plan for our lives that doesn't align with the American dream.

Then Emilio touched on why the service still felt American in many ways, as did many of the church websites I'd browsed before our trip. "Brazilians tend to imitate American culture," he said, "without much filter. That goes for Christians as well, so practices, ideas, and theology, good and bad, are assimilated without much reflection. Every trend in American culture and the American Church will soon find its way into Brazil." Hearing this was both encouraging and terrifying, because American culture and American Christian culture both have produced some amazing things, but we've also produced *Keeping Up with the Kardashians* and Christian T-shirts that rip off every fast-food restaurant logo. It serves as a good reminder to us all to be careful what we produce, because the world is watching and imitating.

■ ■ ■

When I travel, adrenaline usually carries me through the first day, but the second morning always gets me. Our room in Brazil was just dark enough, and the pillows were just soft enough, that sleeping until 3:00 p.m. was a distinct possibility. But we were in the country for only a few days, so we groggily downed a few more cups of Brazilian coffee and took a taxi to the bottom of Corcovado Mountain. At 2,329 feet, Corcovado stands out, even among the other peaks that make Rio so spectacular. But it's the 130-foot statue of Jesus, *Cristo Redentor* or Christ the Redeemer, that makes this one of the New Seven Wonders of the World.

At 9:30 lines were already forming, and after a forty-five-minute wait, we were on one of the rickety trains winding their way up Corcovado. The morning was cloudy, and quickly we climbed into the clouds, where there were no stunning vistas, just a sea of gray. It's a little disconcerting to keep going up, but not being able to see what's ahead of you. Occasionally we'd pass through a break in the clouds, and I'd notice the train was perched on the edge of the world, with nothing between us and the abyss. I shut my eyes and waited until we'd stopped at the top.

Corcovado is part of the Tijuca Forest, a rainforest home to all sorts of creatures not native to Alabama, including monkeys, which were everywhere. Walking from the train past the first food stand, we noticed monkeys on the roof begging for food, and sometimes getting it, from a daring tourist. A couple of Australian girls stood next to us watching in amazement as men passed potato chips to the grateful primates. "You know," I said, "this is how every virus-outbreak movie begins." The Australians agreed, and we left before contracting Motaba virus.

We kept climbing stairs into the gray nothingness until there were no more stairs to climb, and then we saw it, or at least its silhouette. Christ the Redeemer, taller than Godzilla, his head not even visible through the fog. We walked around him a couple of times, craning our necks up at the ghostly figure, then found a place to stand against the viewing platform wall. On a clear day, we would have had one of the most spectacular panoramic views on earth, but today all we could do was watch hundreds of disappointed people looking up at the massive concrete Savior in the haze.

The air on Corcovado was cool, and when a thick cloud blew through, we were covered with a chilly mist. We stood there for an hour or so, with nowhere else to go, when off to the south we noticed a patch of blue sky. Then, in the twinkling of an eye, Christ the Redeemer emerged from the clouds. The crowds went slightly insane, screaming and pointing and desperately trying to pose for photographs in front of the reclusive Son of God. Shut your eyes and you'd have thought Jesus himself had returned to Brazil. And as quickly as he appeared, Christ the Redeemer returned to the clouds. Some people booed.[6] Tricia and I spent three more hours on Corcovado, eating lunch, dodging monkeys,

6. Some people being Tricia.

and enjoying the otherworldly weather, but judging by the silence atop the mountain, Christ the Redeemer, like Boo Radley, would not come out.

Now we were in full tourist mode, so we took a taxi to Sugarloaf Mountain, Rio's other famous peak. Sugarloaf, as you may recall from James Bond's *Moonraker*, is accessed by glass-paneled cable cars. We paid R$30, boarded the next car, and nervously ascended the mountain, because as you will also recall from *Moonraker*, the cables are so thin they can be bitten in two by men with metal teeth. Thankfully no such men were in Rio this day, and we made it safely to the top.

By now the morning clouds had mostly dissipated, and what were left only accented the beautiful sunset. From atop Sugarloaf you have a 360-degree panorama of beaches, mountains, islands, oceans, bays, and the city, sparkling in the setting sun.

We spent the better part of three hours atop Sugarloaf waiting for the sun to set behind the mountains, and once it did, Christ the Redeemer began to glow atop Corcovado. Well, he didn't actually glow—they put floodlights on him—but still, to see a massive, glowing Christ with arms outstretched, standing high above the city, was perhaps the most breathtaking thing I'd ever seen. And I know it's only concrete and rebar, but when you read in Revelation about the city that does not need the sun because it's lit by the glory of God, well, you can't help but think Rio is a little glimpse of heaven.

■ ■ ■

Despite our lifelong Protestantism, we woke up Sunday morning and went to Mass. We were on a tour to see how Christianity is done abroad, after all. On our taxi ride through Botafogo, we passed hundreds, if not thousands, of Brazilians playing soccer—on the beach, on hard courts, on grass fields. I suppose these were recreational leagues of some sort, and I got the feeling we may have been looking at the true national religion of Brazil.

We reached the Catedral Metropolitana de Sao Sebastiao a few minutes before ten, which is when we believed Mass would begin, though the website we'd found wasn't exactly clear. The seat of the archbishop of Rio de Janeiro, the Metropolitan Cathedral looks a bit like a futuristic pyramid whose top has been knocked off. Inside, four stained-glass windows soar from the ground to the ceiling, 246 feet above, and the design in the walls gives you the impression you've stumbled into an oversized beehive. The cathedral has standing room for twenty thousand worshipers, though that much room would not be needed today. A few hundred people, mostly children, were already seated in the two sections in front of the altar, and we took our seats farther back to stay out of the way.

We were handed a program in Portuguese, which, as I've mentioned, we do not speak or read, but still we were able to somewhat keep up with the order of the Mass. First a choir perched high above the altar sang a song that sounded a lot like "O God, Our Help in Ages Past," which was followed by an hour of sitting, standing, repeating, and more singing, until we came to the word *homilia* in the program. "Surely the homily won't take long," I whispered to Tricia. I figured since the service was already running long by my Methodist standards, there was no way this robed priest was going to talk for more than a few minutes, but after half an hour he was still going strong. Tricia leaned over and whispered, "What's the Portuguese word for long-winded?"

By far the strangest thing about the service were the tourists. Not tourists like us who were sitting through the service, but shorts and T-shirt tourists who kept walking in the four massive doors, whispering loudly, and taking pictures, seemingly oblivious to the worship service going on in front of them. At times more than fifty tourists were milling around the edges of the cathedral, and there were always at least a dozen of them standing near the doors.

Sitting there, I made assumptions about the Catholic faith. It is dead, I thought, and the only people they can get to come to Mass are children who have no choice and tourists who don't care. And just then a man walked past us in a number 13 Müller German National Team jersey. He looked every bit the disrespectful tourist, and I thought for a moment he was going to walk up and try to pose for a photograph with the priest. But the man took a seat in front of us, then dropped to his knees and began to pray fervently. Then he stood and joined the line to take Communion, and once he was done, he walked out past us into the street.

A few weeks after I returned home, I asked my friends on Facebook if they'd ever worshiped in a foreign country, and my few Catholic friends said they made it a point to go to Mass whenever they were on vacation. I've never made it a point to worship on vacation, and here I was calling another branch of the faith dead. It's great to be reminded we are not experts on the things we know nothing about.

■ ■ ■

Andrew from River Church kindly offered to take us to lunch a few days later on our last afternoon in Brazil. We went to Fogo de Chão, a Brazilian steak house in Botafogo, although in Brazil I suppose they are just called steak houses. The deal here is you get a card that is red on one side, green on the other, and if you place the card green side up, men will continue to pile slices of beef, pork, poultry, and other sundry animals on your plate until the stack reaches the ceiling. Flip your card over to red, and the men will stand aside as you attempt to eat the skyscraper of meat in front of you. It was one of the greatest hours of my life, and between bites I tried to ask Andrew questions about Christian life in Brazil.

"It's a very spiritual country," he said, cutting up a filet mignon. "These surveys will come out and you learn 85 percent of the country consider themselves Christian, and that 85 percent of the country is poor. It's not like in Alabama, where the wealthy businessmen are also leaders in the church. You don't see church as a networking place like you sometimes do back home."

"Do you prefer this?" I asked Andrew. "Would you rather be planting a church in such a spiritual place, as opposed to, say, Western Europe, where attitudes toward spiritual things are maybe a little cooler?"

Andrew thought for a second, or maybe he was trying to chew his food, then said, "I do love Europe, but each part of the world has a unique set of challenges. Brazil is very spiritual, but there is also this pervading culture of guilt."

I'd noticed this when Andrew spoke a few nights before at River Church. He kept coming back to the fact that it is okay if you miss church one week, and it is okay if you have a beer with dinner; we are not going to condemn each other for these things. "Another challenge," he said, "is that the highest percentage of Protestants in Brazil classify themselves as unchurched. So not only do we want to reach the lost, we want to reach believers and bring them into a loving Christian community. So sure, I would love to plant a church in Europe, but we have a lot of work to do here."

It was raining that night when we boarded our plane, and low-hanging clouds blotted out the city lights just after takeoff. But as we continued to rise, we broke through the clouds and into a clear South American night. And that's when we saw it, off in the distance atop Corcovado, Christ the Redeemer, his glory lighting the city, his outstretched arms calling us back. I watched out the window until the statue finally faded into the night, then I shut my eyes, wondering if I'd ever see it again.

■ ■ ■

"Mr. Gibbs?"

"Huh?"

"Your reason for visiting Brazil?"

Apparently I had not answered quickly enough, and I knew armed guards would soon be escorting me to an interrogation room, where electrodes would be attached to my toes. I guess I could have told him about the warm, loving people we'd met in Brazil, including those of River Church, whose simple goal is to transform the planet for Christ. I could have told him about the barefoot children playing soccer in the street outside our hotel or the barefoot children selling soda on the highway. I could have told him about drinking coconut water through straws, or about the steak house or the monkeys or the rain forest or the Speedos or the glowing Savior standing high above the city at night, his outstretched arms calling me back. I could have told him about Brazil until he was sick of hearing about it, but I didn't.

"It was just a vacation," I said, and he handed back my passport.

But it was the beginning of so much more.

SPAIN

Well I never been to Spain,
but I kinda like the music.

—Three Dog Night,
"Never Been to Spain"

If this book were a ship, then Spain would be a stowaway. Not to say I wasn't planning to visit the Kingdom on the Iberian Peninsula; I just had no intention of writing about the visit. My friend Jordan Ross, whom Tricia blames for my growing love of soccer, and I simply wanted to watch an FC Barcelona match, eat some tapas, then travel to England for the next chapter of this book, a book Zondervan had recently agreed to publish. But travel will surprise you, and oftentimes the unplanned moments are the ones you remember most.

We flew to Madrid, via Miami, on Tuesday, February 7. The flight path took us directly across the Atlantic Ocean, and during the middle of the night, the plane began acting like a giant shake weight. The captain, who, if memory serves me correctly, was crying, asked all the flight attendants to buckle up, and I watched them rush up and down the aisles, one of them falling over into some seats during a particularly nasty bump. And while I was thinking of sins I could give up as a bargaining chip with God, Jordan, who is an engineer and shouldn't believe in things like this, leaned over and said, "Wouldn't we be over the Bermuda Triangle right about now?" I ignored this question and continued praying until the fasten seat belts sign dinged off a few minutes later, at which point I acted like nothing had happened and resumed reading Hemingway's *Death in the Afternoon.*

We landed around 9:00 a.m., and after a brief stare down with an incredibly bored immigration agent, Jordan and I were out of Madrid's futuristic airport and on the metro, making our way downtown. Through some rather poor planning on my part, we had about forty-seven minutes to explore Madrid, and as any seasoned traveler will tell you, you need at least an hour to see it all. So we decided to catch the Plaza Mayor and the Royal Palace and miss whatever was left.

We hopped off at Puerta del Sol, Madrid's Times Square, and I quickly realized I had no idea which direction we should walk, so I activated international data on my phone and pulled up Google Maps. Within seconds I began receiving one text message after another.

"You have exceeded $50 in international roaming charges."
"You have exceeded $100 in international roaming charges."

"You have exceeded $150 in international roaming charges."
"You have exceeded the GDP of Canada in international roaming charges."
"You have somehow exceeded ∞ in international roaming charges."

"I can loan you twenty bucks, if that will help," Jordan said, but again I ignored him. I knew I had purchased an international data package, but these texts were too scary to ignore, so I called my phone company and a nice lady told me that sometimes the system doesn't recognize the new data plan immediately, and that I did not owe them $1,946,424,394, as my phone suggested. I thanked her, then pulled up Google Maps again, and soon Jordan and I were standing in the Plaza Mayor, which was empty because it was thirty-two degrees.

Slightly disappointed and considerably freezing, we walked on farther to the Royal Palace of Madrid, which is the official residence of Juan Carlos I, the king of Spain. Juan Carlos and his family don't actually live in the palace, because at 1,450,000 square feet, it's possible the king could get lost on his way to the bathroom and never be seen again. Instead the king and his family live at the Palace of Zarzuela, which is a more modest 33,900 square feet. The Royal Palace, best we could tell from the twenty frostbitten minutes we stared at it, was built primarily as a means to attract gawking foreigners.

Then our forty-seven minutes were up and we had to rush to Atocha Station to catch our train to Barcelona. These train tickets cost us $120, and I still am not sure if they were a good deal. That's because Spaniards, like the rest of Europe, use the metric system, a scale of measurements designed specifically to confuse Americans. I tried to calculate the price of a train versus the price of renting a car by creating a word problem, but this only managed to give me a headache.

> Suppose Chad has $120 and wants to travel the 384 miles from Madrid to Barcelona, leaving him enough money to buy tapas for dinner. Keeping in mind that there are 1.609 kilometers in a mile, and that one dollar is worth .7601 euros, and that fuel in Spain is called petrol, not gasoline, and that stations sell it by the litre, not the

gallon, and the Europeans spell liter with the *r* and *e* reversed, and that Chad isn't entirely sure he can legally drive in Spain, how many tapas can Chad eat in one sitting?

See what I mean? There is simply no way to know which is cheaper. The train was nice, though, and the seats reclined just enough, and as much as I wanted to enjoy the scenic trip across eastern Spain, I wanted to sleep even more. Four hours later, I woke up on the outskirts of Barcelona.

I don't recall how we got from Barcelona's Sants Station to our hotel on Gran Via de les Corts Catalanes. I'm assuming we took the metro, but it's a bit of a blur, and in my notes from this part of the trip, I have only the words "Grt Ati Aroport," which isn't helpful. At the hotel, we napped and showered, and around 8:00 p.m., we headed out to watch the Barcelona versus Valencia match that started at 9:00 p.m., which seemed a little late to me, but from what I gathered during my stay there, time doesn't really work in Spain the way it works in America.

Speaking of time, I learned quickly that I needed to have patience on my travels or I would go insane. The United States is considered a monochromic society, meaning we value a strict schedule, view time as a resource, equate time with money, and get rather annoyed when we think someone is wasting our time. There are cultures that share this view of time, but the US is on one extreme end of the spectrum. So when we find ourselves in a country where services don't begin when they are supposed to or trains don't arrive on schedule or the freaking waiter won't even bring me my bill, we have to remember these things aren't meant as personal slights;[1] they are just parts of a different culture.

The next day was wide open, and Jordan and I planned to see as much of the city as possible. First stop was Sagrada Família, a Catholic church designed by Antoni Gaudí, who is not to be confused with Antoni Gaudy, who I guess would have insisted that the outside of the church be bedazzled. The church didn't look like any church I'd ever

1. Unless you are wearing one of those "USA: Back-to-Back World War Champs" T-shirts; then it may actually be a personal slight.

seen, mostly because I've never seen churches on other planets. The front facade, or maybe it's the rear facade, it was hard to tell, looks like it is made of melting wax. Despite the fact construction began in 1882, the church is still not finished. In 2011 officials announced construction would wrap up in 2026, or maybe 2028. Spaniards, it seems, are in a hurry only when being chased by bulls.

For me the strangest thing about Sagrada Familía, apart from the way it looks, is that I'm not sure who will worship there once it's finished. There are many cathedrals in Europe that now function primarily as tourist attractions. Thing is, those other cathedrals at some point were busy, functioning churches. In what many are calling post-Christian Spain, it seems by the time Sagrada Familía is finished, it will be a church that was always a tourist attraction first.

As in most of Western Europe, Christianity is declining in Spain. A 2011 study showed that 70.1 percent of the country identify themselves as Catholic, but another study showed a significantly lower percentage of Spaniards actually believe in God. This leads you to believe that for many in Spain, Catholicism is more heritage than something they practice.

As Jordan and I slowly walked around Sagrada Familía, lamenting the fact that more churches back home aren't designed by extraterrestrials, I began to wonder how much of our Christianity in the Bible Belt has become about heritage as well. Church attendance figures on Easter and Christmas suggest that for many, Christianity is just another tradition, though church attendance is certainly not a perfect barometer of one's faith. But my home state of Alabama has a population of 4.8 million, and in most polls, around 90 percent of Alabamians claim to be Christian. However, there are more than twelve hundred children waiting to be adopted in Alabama's foster care program. My wife and I have the resources to adopt one of these children, as do thousands, if not tens of thousands, of Alabamians, yet we don't. And standing there in the shadow of Gaudí's masterpiece, a frightening thought occurred to me. What will I tell my son when he reads the Gospels and asks why we never adopted an orphan? "Because, son, we needed that spare bedroom for guests on football weekends." Is there an answer I can give him that won't cause disillusionment? There's nothing wrong with having a Christian heritage, but when our faith becomes a box we check on surveys, and not a life we live, we shouldn't act surprised when the next generation says, "No, thanks."

■ ■ ■

We spent the afternoon in the Old City, smelling saltwater in the Mediterranean breeze and strolling down La Rambla, a street whose name literally means "the Boulevard" and figuratively means "the Tourist Trap." We wanted tapas and perused the sidewalk cafes, comparing the chalk menus until we settled on a place that was serving two tapas and a pasta dish for €5. We sat down, pointed at two tapas each on the picture menu, and both ordered seafood paella for the main course. The tapas were okay, but the paella, topped with shrimp and mussels straight from the Mediterranean, was so tasty I still dream about it. I was tempted to call it the greatest cheap lunch I'd ever had, but the chalk menu failed to mention we'd be paying an additional €7 for a few lukewarm milliliters of Coca-Cola. Stupid metric system.

After lunch we wandered aimlessly through the Old City, stopping to visit Barcelona Cathedral, an enormous five-hundred-year-old Gothic church. Then we toured the Picasso Museum, to enjoy the works of an artist who occasionally depicts noses with triangles. Then we went to a Bible study. I know, kind of random.

Even though we were visiting Spain only for a soccer match, in the weeks before the trip, I couldn't resist searching for Christian organizations in Barcelona to see if something was going on that Jordan and I could attend. The first church I found is called the International Church of Barcelona, and their primary goal is reaching out to the English-speaking community of Barcelona, and I thought, Hey, I speak English, so I sent them an email. Turned out there was a young adults' Bible study the last night we were in town, and the leaders, John and Brandi, said they'd love to have us.

Thanks to some confusion on the train, we arrived in the Les Planes neighborhood of Barcelona thirty minutes late for the Bible study. "Do you think that's the place?" Jordan asked, pointing at a large white building up the hill. "I guess," I said, and we walked over to investigate.

The big white building on the hill looked a lot like someone's house when we finally reached it, and I hated to knock, because it was unlikely the person who lived there spoke English, but I also hated to snoop around, because the police arresting us for trespassing were just as unlikely to speak English. Jordan knocked and no one answered, but in their defense, he didn't knock hard. Then we walked down some stairs to the back of the house, where we surprised a man walking outside to make a phone call.

"Uh," I eloquently began, "we're looking for John and Brandi."

"Brandi is inside," he said and pointed toward the door he'd just exited.

We walked in and stood in the doorway. The study had obviously not begun, as people of all races and nationalities were standing around, drinking coffee, and conversing in various languages and accents, some of which I'm pretty sure are illegal in Alabama. We didn't know what to do or who to talk to, but then a woman near the front of the room shouted our names and said, "Welcome! You guys come and get your name tags."

It was Brandi, and she began taking us around the room to introduce us to members of the group. I told her I thought we were late, and she said, "Eight thirty really means nine here, at the earliest."

Jordan and I grabbed some snacks and sat down, and soon we were talking to Kelsey Beckman, a young American from Kansas. "How'd you end up living in Barcelona?" I asked her.

"Have you heard of El Camino de Santiago?" she asked.

I had. In English it's called the Way of St. James, and though there are numerous routes, the most famous is the five-hundred-mile trek across northern Spain, from Saint-Jean-Pied-de-Port on the French side of the Pyrenees Mountains, all the way to Santiago de Compostela, where the remains of St. James are supposedly buried. Pilgrims have been making this journey for centuries, and they still are today. Nearly two hundred thousand of them walked (or biked) the Way in 2011.

"You did that?" I asked, more jealous than anything else, because Tricia said I couldn't do it without her, and that she didn't want to do it. But if I were, let's say, a twenty-one-year-old college student reading this book, I'd put this book down and start researching the Way of St. James for my graduation trip.[2]

"It was, hands down, the greatest experience of my life," Kelsey said. "The whole point of my pilgrimage was to have thirty-plus days completely focused on God and his will for my life, without all the stressors and crap that get in the way of that focus daily."

"Do you think that was why most pilgrims were there?"

"I met some people who were there for the same reasons, but I think more were just doing it for fun. I even met one guy from Australia who said he was afraid he'd meet all these intense Catholics and hardcore Bible thumpers on the Way. I found it kind of odd that people would participate in a centuries old religious tradition hoping not to encounter anything religious. But to each his own, I guess."

"So you made the pilgrimage, fell in love with Spain, and decided to stay?"

"I met a guy too."

"Aah. So what's it like being a Christian in Spain?"

"Way different than I would have imagined," Kelsey said. "Even though Spain is technically a Catholic country, I have met only atheists. And they are proud to be so. People just can't understand how I can be twenty-six and a believer. They see Christianity as something ancient and dead. Something that has no place in the world today, especially for people my age. And they don't just ask if I'm a Christian and drop it when I say yes; they talk about all of the horrible things the church has done throughout history. It can be immensely frustrating, but it has also really challenged me and deepened my faith. At first I was always on the defensive, but eventually I realized that living out my faith and being an example would have way more impact than arguing."

Cesar, a thirty-five-year-old Barcelona native, told me a similar story. "In secondary school, friends would laugh at me when I said I was

2. What are you waiting for? Put this book down.

an evangelical Christian. Young people here are rather agnostic. They don't know about God, and they are not really interested to find out."[3]

Listening to Kelsey and Cesar, it dawned on me that I cannot recall ever being laughed at for my beliefs, never mind facing persecution. In the Bible Belt, it is still tougher to admit you are *not* a person of faith. Back home, Christianity is our default setting. In contrast, Spaniards my age were born into a dictatorship where Roman Catholicism was the only religion with legal status, so it doesn't make much sense to compare the United States and Spain, but it does perhaps shed some light on some of their less than positive views on the church. And as I chatted with Kelsey and Cesar, I wondered about the different reasons a society might turn away from Christianity. Spaniards appear to have revolted against a heavy-handed, authoritarian church. Will the next generation of Americans turn away from complacent comfortable Christianity? Is this why millennials in America are already leaving the church?

At the Bible study, Jordan and I met more Americans, a guy from Brazil, some Germans, some Chinese, perhaps a Vulcan, and even a few Spaniards. Brandi's husband, John, came in with their young daughter, Anabelle, a little later, and Jordan and I spoke to them for a few minutes.

"Christianity is different here in many ways," Brandi began. "Take alcohol. Here there is no issue with alcohol; it's even served at pastors' gatherings. Our young adults constantly ask us to go out for a beer after service. Girls here, Christian or not, wear whatever they want. Modesty isn't talked about like it is back home. And many of our Christian friends curse frequently and see no issue with it at all."

The study began, and Brandi had me come up front to introduce me to the group in Spanish. It's very strange to stand in front of a group of strangers while someone talks about you in a foreign language. I did catch the words "Dios y futbol" as she held up the copy of my first book, *God and Football*, which I'd brought them. Then she explained the book was about American football, and there were groans from the soccer-loving crowd.

---

3. Cesar also told me that now many Latin Americans are arriving in Spain and spreading the gospel—the Latin Americans whose ancestors heard the Good News from the Spanish.

As they spoke that night, John in English, Brandi in Spanish, I couldn't help but scan the room, looking at faces from around the world. I loved it. We were not divided by countries or by race, but we were all of God's children, together. When the lesson ended, Brandi prayed in Spanish, which I do not speak, but I was nevertheless moved every time I heard her say Señor, a Spanish word for God.

As the group departed to catch the next train back to Barcelona, Jordan and I said goodbye to Brandi and John. I told them how much I'd enjoyed Spain and explained the thoughts behind this book a little more.

"I'm a wired skeptic," Brandi said. "I joke with John that I often flow in the 'gift of disbelief.' In the States, there was enough Christian culture to propel me along. I was in constant church services, Bible studies, girls' groups, Sunday school, fellowship nights—just constant. This created a dichotomy. I was trapped, and I was safe. I couldn't deal with the real thoughts going through my head, yet I was in the current enough to be lulled along from week to week to still 'be good and live for God.'"

"And living here?" I asked.

"Living in Europe, all of those safeguards are gone. There's no one dragging you to church. There's no commitment to read the Word or pray. There's no weekly structure that will keep you on the straight and narrow. Here you have to want it, and you have to fight for it. Living here has opened my mind and eyes, and has been shocking and also liberating. I still maintain most of the 'fundamentals' I was raised with in the US, but I also recognize that my world is not *the* world."

I thought a lot about the things Brandi said as Jordan and I waited at Les Planes station for the train to take us back into Barcelona, and I've thought about them a lot since then. It's important to reflect on how much of my faith is shaped by where I live on a map. I'm thankful to have grown up in Alabama, I truly am, but talking to people who have their faith questioned on a daily basis, I felt keenly aware of how complacent my own faith had become. How complacent most of us have become in the comfortable Bible Belt. I could be wrong here—my next seminary course will be my first—but when I read the New Testament,

I don't see any promises of a comfortable life. I usually see promises of the opposite. But comfortable might be the perfect word to describe life back home. It's really only when people make their lives uncomfortable, by giving away possessions or adopting a bunch of children, that we start questioning them and calling them zealots. I don't want you to think I'm yearning for the days of a post-Christian America, though those days very well may be coming. It's just that Jesus said the world would hate us because of him, and I've never really felt it. Maybe if my Christian life feels comfortable, I'm doing it wrong.

ENGLAND

I saw a werewolf with a Chinese menu in his hand,
walking through the streets of Soho in the rain.

—Warren Zevon, "Werewolves of London"

The next morning, Jordan and I flew from Barcelona to London, both of us marveling at the snow-covered Pyrenees, which we, geography whizzes that we are, both referred to as the Alps. We landed at Gatwick Airport, the Stephen Baldwin to London Heathrow's Alec, then took a crowded train to Victoria Station in central London, where all of the earth's people had apparently just gathered for a flash mob.

The soulful sounds of a jackhammer echoed throughout the station, a booming, Orwellian voice kept reminding us all to "mind the gap," and my overstuffed suitcase and I just wanted to buy a tube pass and get out of everyone's way. But instead Jordan and I found ourselves holding up the ticket line because we had no idea what zone we needed to travel to. Twilight? Auto? It was all so confusing.

Generally speaking, visiting England is much easier than visiting other European countries. This is because they speak English, or at least a form of it that somehow makes them all sound smarter.[1] However, after two minutes inside the mosh pit that is Victoria Station, I was on the brink of a nervous collapse. Finally I hid in a dark corner while Jordan bought our tube passes. An hour later we checked in to our hotel.

By now we felt like the power had blinked and our internal clocks had been flashing 12:00 for who knows how long, so we opted for naps over sightseeing, waking in time to make the Friday evensong service at St. Paul's.

St. Paul's Cathedral, named for the apostle, not the Beatle, was founded in 604 AD. Four buildings preceded the one whose Great West Door we found ourselves shivering in front of that February evening, this "newest" version constructed in 1677.

When we stepped into the nave of St. Paul's, our eyes instinctively darted up to the ornate ceiling, down to the black-and-white checkered floor, then behind us to the stern gentleman asking us to please pocket our cameras. As we walked east toward the 225-foot dome, our

1. They do not, however, use the euro, opting instead for something called the pound, a magical currency that, instead of making everything you buy cost 50 percent more, makes everything you buy cost 100 percent more.

footsteps echoed over hushed voices. I reached into my pocket for the third time in a minute, making extra sure my cell phone was on vibrate.

Jordan and I stood under the center of the dome, craning our necks to look up past the Whispering Gallery to the eight paintings of the life of St. Paul. Then we took our seats, neither of us speaking as we continued to gaze at the quire, which is how the Church of England spells choir, which actually makes more sense and is worth a lot more points on Words with Friends.

A month before leaving for England, I spoke to Jason, a friend of a friend and a real-life Englishman. I asked him about Christianity in England over the last one hundred years, and he said, "I think one of the reasons the church in England is perhaps losing popularity is that it's perceived as being, I suppose, somewhat hypocritical, in that they have a message of reaching out to the least among us, and yet at the same time they are harboring vast wealth."

I certainly understood the tension in what Jason said. I've heard similar grumbles from church members over new multi-million-dollar building campaigns, so I can imagine how the unchurched members of the community must view us. When I read books like *Radical* by David Platt, I began to feel guilty that the church has ever spent one dime on a building. I cringe at the thought of ten-million-dollar building campaigns when there are so many people starving to death. But when I sit in a breathtaking church like St. Paul's and I marvel at the masterpiece of architects and artisans, some of whom worshiped God through their craft, I have trouble feeling the guilt I have toward modern buildings. Perhaps this is hypocritical, but perhaps I'm a hypocrite.

During the service, I felt the chill bumps on my arms as the words to the Magnificat echoed through what, for 252 years, was the tallest building in London. And I grew a little misty-eyed as I heard my own cracking voice joining the multitudes who for centuries have said, "As it was in the beginning, is now, and ever shall be, world without end. Amen."

The beautiful service lasted an hour and included, of all things, a prayer for the Diocese of Arkansas, which elicited bewildered glances between Jordan and me, both of us half-expecting the pastor to lead us in calling the hogs. Afterward we ate at an Italian restaurant across the street and between bites of pizza briefly pondered the theological ramifications of our asking God to save the queen, but mostly we talked about soccer. Then, before retiring to our hotel for the evening, we made a quick stop at Piccadilly Circus, which isn't a circus at all, just a busy road junction, but hey, at least there were no clowns.

■ ■ ■

Tricia believes I am convinced that the constraints of space and time do not apply to me while traveling. She constantly has to remind me there is not enough time in the day to see and do all of the things I think should be seen and done. Unfortunately for me, and especially for Jordan, Tricia did not help plan this trip to London, which is why at 5:00 a.m. on Saturday morning the alarm rudely began our day.

Two hours later, as our train slowly crept out from Paddington Station, Jordan woke up enough to ask the obvious question: "Why did we have to take such an early train?"

Regrettably, the obvious question did not have an equally obvious answer. Truth is, a 7:00 a.m. train didn't seem that early when I booked it two months earlier, in the middle of the afternoon. Hearing this, I figured, would only make Jordan resent me for the rest of the day, so I shrugged and said, "You'll have to ask Tricia; she booked it."

Our early departure was made even less pleasant by the fact that England was waking up from the coldest night of the winter, with temperatures dipping into the middle teens. We both shivered while gazing out the window at field after field covered in snow, where even the horses were wearing thick wool blankets.

An hour later, we were at the Oxford railway station, which is half a mile west of the city of Oxford. We quickly walked down Botley Road, hands in pockets, teeth chattering. And unlike C. S. Lewis, who on his first visit to the City of Dreaming Spires apparently left the station going the wrong way and actually walked to Botley, we walked straight to Oxford, stopping at the first coffee shop we saw.

Inside, I studied the menu so that, like Jay Gatsby, I could one day tell people I studied at Oxford, then ordered a tall cup of hot coffee. And sitting in an upstairs booth overlooking a row of old brick buildings on empty George Street, Jordan asked the next obvious question: "Now, what exactly are we doing here?"

We were in Oxford to go to a pub. But not just any pub; we were going to the Eagle and Child, where C. S. Lewis, J. R. R. Tolkien, and a group of Oxford literary types who called themselves the Inklings met weekly to discuss literature, read from their unfinished works, and, I suppose, guess what each other's initials stood for. However, the Eagle and Child did not open until 11:00 a.m., so we had a little time on our hands.

We finished our coffee and walked into town, turning in the direction of the largest cathedral spire we could see. It was Christ Church, one of the larger colleges of the University of Oxford and the cathedral of the Diocese of Oxford. We walked around the cathedral to the playing fields and Christ Church Meadow, both of which were covered in a frozen layer of snow. Our feet crunched beneath us, and we decided the £8.50 tour was worth it to get out of the cold.

Inside, we walked through the Great Hall, the inspiration for the Great Hall at Hogwarts in the Harry Potter films. Unfortunately, none of the portraits in Christ Church's Great Hall moved.

The Boy Who Lived is not the only piece of children's literature inspired by Christ Church. The people and places around Oxford and Christ Church inspired much of Lewis Carroll's *Alice in Wonderland.* Alice's rabbit hole symbolized the stairs in the back of the Great Hall.

From there we walked back down St. Aldate's, through a narrow canyon of buildings, some older than the United States, then up High Street and its yet-to-open shops, before making our way over to Broad Street and Blackwell's, a 120-year-old book shop, where we had our second of three cups of coffee that chilly morning.

Finally the bell towers around Oxford rang the eleventh hour, and we made our way over to the Eagle and Child for lunch. Nicknamed the Bird and Baby, and sometimes simply called the Bird, the pub is housed in a three-story building on St. Giles. The sign out front depicts an eagle carrying, or perhaps kidnapping, a swaddled baby. Historically, pubs had signs like these, such as the one across the street adorned with a lamb and flag, because many of their patrons could not read.

Inside, we passed on the meat pies and ordered fish and chips with a dark beer that wasn't quite as life changing as our waiter had hinted, then we took a table just off the Rabbit Room, where the Inklings once met. I felt the literary energy of the place, where once upon a time, for instance, early drafts of *The Lord of the Rings* and *The Lion, the Witch, and the Wardrobe* had been read aloud by their creators. Not having any masterpieces of our own to read aloud, Jordan and I just listened to the radio playing Train's "Hey, Soul Sister," all but ruining the moment.

As Jordan and I ate our fish and chips in contemplative silence, I wondered what Lewis would think of American Christianity, because we seem to think a lot of him. American pastors who disagree on everything agree you can't really write a Christian book these days without quoting him.

> It may be hard for an egg to turn into a bird: it would be a jolly sight harder for a bird to learn to fly while remaining an egg.
>
> —C. S. Lewis, *Mere Christianity*

See what I mean?

My problem, and his too, I suppose, is that C. S. Lewis died fifty years ago, so finding his views on modern American Christianity has proved difficult. However, I was able to talk to Paul, a friend I met on Twitter, of all places, who, despite never being quoted by John Piper or Rob Bell, is British and, I suppose more important, is alive.

"I'm personally very impressed by the general optimism and spirit that seems to come with the American dream. There is often a cynicism to English culture, which compares poorly with American aspirations."

I believe Paul is right, and I think in a way the American dream and Christianity go well together. Not the "I need a ninety-inch flat-screen TV in every room and two SUVs in the garage" version of the American dream, but the unfailing optimism of it. We're the nation that saw the moon and said, "Hey, let's play golf up there!" To a cynic, the Great Commission probably sounds like a lot of work. To an optimist, it sounds more like, "I love travel, and God is on our side; what can go wrong?"

"It's good to love your country," Paul continued, "but America is a relatively new nation, historically speaking, and appears to forget it does not have the huge Christian heritage of much of Europe. Christianity is essentially an Eastern religion, coming out of Jerusalem, not Texas. We gentiles are newcomers to God's kingdom, and even this is through his amazing grace, not national superiority."

I sensed that Paul had a point. I wondered if perhaps our eternal optimism combined with our success at moon golf has gone to our heads. I thought back to a time in my life, as a teenager, coming home from summer church camp, all hopped up on God and thinking the older people in our church were fools. I thought they had no idea what it means to be "on fire for God," and I doubted the sincerity of their commitment to Christ. Maybe America, in a way, is Christianity's know-it-all bratty teenager. Or maybe Paul is still a little upset about all that business back in 1776.[2]

By noon the high sun had warmed Oxford enough that the streets were bustling with shoppers, and Jordan and I made one last pass through town on our way to the train that would carry us back to London. That afternoon we saw Fulham beat Stoke City 2-1 at Craven Cottage, and that evening we had dinner with an actual British family.

Some friends from Lakeview Baptist Church in Auburn had suggested I get in touch with Alan and Alyson while in London, because Alan spent some time in Auburn in the early nineties training to be a youth minister, and the two of them have been back to Alabama many times since. I reached out to Alyson, and she was kind enough to invite Jordan and me to dinner on Saturday night, saying we should take the District Line to Earl's Court, then make our way to platform 9 3/4 to take the Piccadilly Line to Northfields, where we'd need to take the E3

2. USA! USA! USA!

bus, hopping off at the Church Road stop, which was around the corner from their house. Easy enough, until we tried it.

"How'd we miss the Church Road stop?" I asked the bus driver, after he'd informed us we were at the end of the line.

"Easy," he said, "there isn't one. At least not anymore."

He told us the name of the stop we were looking for and we hopped off, bought another ticket, hopped back on, then took the bus back through west London, this time getting off when we were supposed to. Minutes later we were knocking on the door to Alan and Alyson's home.

Alyson greeted us warmly at the door and took us inside to meet Alan and their daughter, Hannah. Over dinner we talked about Auburn and travel and soccer, Jordan and I trying to convince Alan to join us in the morning for Aston Villa versus Manchester City. Then sometime after dessert, which consisted of these creamy pastry sandwiches the size of Krystal burgers, our talked turned to faith.

I was interested to talk to Hannah, who is in her early twenties, because growing up in Alabama, the vast majority of the kids I went to school with attended church. Maybe they went only because their parents made them, but they went. Point being, in the Bible Belt it is socially awkward, if not social suicide, to be a confessing nonbeliever.

"Did you have many Christian friends at school?" I asked her.

"I was really the only Christian I knew at school," she said.

I couldn't help but laugh, because the hardest part of being a Christian at my high school was waking up in time for the See You at the Pole rally once a year. I have no concept of what it's like to be the only Christian at your school. How hard it would be to be different in the teenage world of "different is bad." I wondered if I would have just kept all that Jesus stuff to myself in that environment, and probably for the first time, I realized just how easy I'd had it growing up in Alabama.

Paul, my Twitter friend from Manchester, confirmed this. "Personally," he said, "my friends and work colleagues politely tolerate my faith, but my kids have more of a struggle. They are experiencing a generation where belief in God is mocked. My eight-year-old recently had an experience where a schoolteacher explained to the class how the Bible was just an oral history and couldn't be trusted on anything. They are doing well in their personal faith, all things considered, but I do think they will have more of a struggle than I did."

I realize that on the persecution scale, mocked beliefs rank just above kids playing keep-away with your Bible. And I also realize I didn't have to travel all the way across the Atlantic to find a place where it's not easy to be a Christian in school. School in Manchester, England, probably isn't much different from school in Manchester, New Hampshire. Scripture tells us we will be mocked for our beliefs, it prepares us for it, but I grew up in a world where you went to church with your teachers and evolution was taught with the disclaimer "you don't have to believe this, but you have to know it for the test." If a teacher had told our class that the Bible can't be trusted and all around me heads were nodding up and down, would I have nodded too?

As I ate my second of three pastries, Alyson talked about how visiting Christian friends in the States can lead to awkward conversations for her, because the American Church is strongly aligned with right wing politics, while her beliefs tend to lean more, brace yourself, socialist.

Paul told me much the same thing when we spoke later. "It is a constant amazement how Christian faith and right wing politics have become associated. I get the impression I would struggle in certain churches, not for my theology but for my politics, and this surely can't be correct."

I generally loathe political discussion. Every election season I half expect Facebook to call and say, "Mr. Gibbs, you've hidden 97 percent of your friends. Wouldn't you rather we just delete your account?" Part of my discomfort stems from what Paul and Alyson are talking about. A segment of American Christians has reduced every economic and social issue down to two sides, the Christian side and the other side. If your opinion on an issue falls outside what they've determined is the biblical response, your opinions on all other matters are assumed invalid. Life, of course, is more nuanced than this, and there are many Christians who lean left on some issues, yet still lean right on others.

I wondered, reaching for my third dessert pastry, if in the US church we've lost the ability, or maybe the desire, to take part in civil dialogue. I'm not saying we should change our beliefs and convictions, and I'm not saying we should put one of those "coexist" stickers on our cars. But I do think the next time we see some snarky political Facebook post that will anger people who disagree with it, maybe we shouldn't click the share button.

Alan volunteered to drive us back to our hotel that evening, which saved us from having to navigate the bus system again, but introduced me to the terror of being a front seat passenger in England. As Alan sped down side streets and through roundabouts, I instinctively reached for an imaginary steering wheel, stomped on the imaginary brake pedal, and more than once had to restrain myself from grabbing the rearview mirror and turning it in my direction. Driving on the right side of the car may be difficult, but it can't be worse than riding on the left side.[3]

■ ■ ■

Sunday morning Jordan and I were set to attend worship at Holy Trinity Brompton (HTB), a church that describes itself as a "vibrant Anglican church in the heart of London." The service began at 9:30, and we were making good time until we got off at the High Street Kensington stop, not the South Kensington stop we needed. We eventually made it, though, following a mom and her four kids to HTB, which is tucked behind the massive Church of the Immaculate Heart of Mary off the Brompton Road.

HTB's main site, the 183-year-old building we were at, looks like it was on MTV's *Pimp My Cathedral*. The pews had been removed and replaced with comfortable chairs, sound and lighting equipment hung from the ceiling, flat-screen televisions were mounted on columns throughout the space, and above the altar a large video screen displayed worship lyrics and promotional videos for church events. It felt like any other contemporary church back home, except for the wraparound

3. FYI, this is not a political statement. I'm talking about the left and right seats in the car.

balcony, the stained-glass windows, and the colorfully ornate woodwork on the ceiling. Visually, it is perhaps the most interesting church I've ever attended.

Speaking of attending, some pretty famous people attend HTB, one being Bear Grylls, the deodorant salesman who purposely gets lost in the woods. Rumor has it the lads from Mumford and Sons attend HTB as well and have even led worship, though the lack of YouTube videos leaves me skeptical of the leading worship part.

After a loud and lively time of worship led by a praise band armed with electric guitars, and a video promo for Focus, an upcoming Christian festival at the beach that looked like a mix between a Passion conference and Woodstock, Associate Vicar Nicky Lee began a sermon series on transforming relationships. He preached from Genesis 1:26–27, and while I'm certain the sermon was excellent, my notes from that morning only say, "I wish my pastor had a British accent."

Scanning the large crowd that morning, I wasn't expecting to see such a vibrant, thriving church in the heart of London. I'd read so many articles about "spiritually dead Europe" that it was hard not to think of everyone on that side of the Atlantic as agnostics who own Bibles only for emergency kindling. I was reminded of a conversation I had with my friend Shawn Smucker, a writer from Pennsylvania who lived in England for four years before returning to the States. Shawn and his wife were part of a small Baptist congregation in the town of Aylesbury, and I asked him about living in a place where he felt like part of the minority.

"It caused two things," Shawn said. "First of all, we had a lot of friends outside of the church. Second, we became more intent on going to church, not out of a sense of duty but because there, in that little gathering, were the only people in your life who truly understood you. Many of our fellow churchgoers were the only believers in their family or at their work or among their friends. This didn't keep them from having deep relationships with those people, but church was the only place they could go to interact with other believers, so it was special."

Christianity is still the majority religion in England, though according to polls, only a very small percentage of that majority consider themselves practicing Christians. And I suppose those of us living in the Bible Belt tend to look at minority Christianity as somehow failing Christianity, especially in a country with freedom of religion, like England, even though Christ seemed to spend a lot of time preparing us to be part of the minority. But now when I think of Christianity in England, I think of Holy Trinity Brompton and other churches like it. I think of small pockets of believers living out their faith, encouraging one another, and trying to shine the light of Christ in a dark world. I think of that mom walking her four sons to church on a cold London morning. I think of all these things, and I am filled with hope.

I was telling Jordan this after the service while shaking hands and enjoying some of HTB's free coffee. I wouldn't say I want church attendance back home to resemble England's, but I do believe majority Christianity makes it easy to just go through the motions. Going through the motions is almost a requirement. But in England there doesn't seem to be any benefit of being a lukewarm believer; you get all the ridicule without the benefits. My friend Shawn said in England he stopped going to church out of duty, and started going because the fellowship was special. It's sad, but sometimes back home I fear we go to church not so much to encounter God but to encounter those who would make it a point to mention they didn't encounter us at church last Sunday. I'm neither God nor a cardiologist, so I couldn't look into the hearts of everyone at Holy Trinity Brompton that morning. However, I got the feeling that they were there to experience God in a loving Christian fellowship, not because it would look bad if they slept in.

■ ■ ■

After the service at HTB, we rushed across town to catch a train to Birmingham, where we would watch my favorite soccer club, Manchester City, take on the home side, Aston Villa.

We didn't have much time to wander around the birthplace of Ozzy Osbourne. Long enough for me to pose for a photograph in front of St.

Chad's Cathedral,[4] and just long enough to realize the last three letters of the city's name are pronounced *um*, not *ham* like back home. Although I seriously doubt they would call a ham sandwich an um sandwich.

City won the match 1-0, and after dinner at a fine local establishment, Pizza Hut, we boarded a late night train back to London, both of us trying to sleep but waking suddenly every ten minutes when the train stopped at a new station, each one sounding exponentially more British than the last—Coventry, Stony Stratford, Leighton Buzzard, Holes in Blackburn Lancashire, Um Sandwich.

The next morning, we were up early for our flight back home, and as we were walking down the bustling streets of Hammersmith and Fulham to ride the tube one last time, we passed dozens of English schoolchildren, many of them wearing ties and jackets, some in knee-socks and shorts like that AC/DC guitarist. I wondered if any of them were Christians or came from Christian homes, and I wondered what kind of England they would grow up in. Then I thought about something Alyson said about the Bible Belt as we were leaving her house a few nights earlier. She said, "I think Christianity in the United States is about fifty years behind England."

A part of me is fearful when I hear that, but only because I've lived my entire life in a comfortable place where Christians are an overwhelming majority. But after this trip to England, a part of me is hopeful too, because I was reminded that wherever there are people who love God, God is at work. Sure, Christianity isn't booming in England, but there are pockets, vibrant, thriving pockets of genuine Christian community. Perhaps Christianity has become too easy back home and in fifty years that comfortable chaff will be burned away. Being a Christian in England isn't easy, and I doubt the next five decades will be as easy for Christians in America, but nobody said this was supposed to be easy.

4. No relation.

RUSSIA

I've traveled the world to learn,
I must return from Russia with love.
—Lionel Bart, "From Russia with Love"

It's not their fault.

The good people of Russia cannot help that for the past fifty years or so, they've been portrayed as the bad guys in our films. They cannot help that when I hear someone speak English with a Russian accent, I think of Ivan Drago or some nameless commando parachuting into Colorado to kill Patrick Swayze and his friends. They can't help it, but at this point neither can I, so when the young woman at the front desk of Moscow's Best Western Vega Hotel and Conference Center said, "Standard room. You receive *no* breakfast," she sounded to me probably a little more sinister than she was.

Just getting to Moscow had been an adventure. I'd invited my old friend Ryan Cothran, whom I'd met in second grade when I asked him to join my bird club,[1] to travel with me to Russia because he's an elementary school teacher and has summers off. I probably hadn't spoken to Ryan in six months when I called and said, "So, would you like to go with me to Moscow?"

"Not really," he said, but I threatened to tell the world about his high school line-dancing obsession and he relented.

Weeks later as we settled in for the long trans-Atlantic flight, we were greeted with news from the flight deck that our plane's fuel pump or wing or something had broken, and we needed to return to the gate for repairs. The delay caused us to miss our connection in Dusseldorf and cost us four of our twenty-four hours in Paris, and apparently created an alternate universe, a universe where Air France had no record of our being on their flight to Moscow the following morning. Arguing with the French ticket agent was one of the top five most stressful moments of my life—the other four all involved parking at church—but things were finally straightened out, and a few hours later we landed at Moscow's Sheremetyevo International Airport, which is pronounced just like it's spelled, I guess.

By googling "Moscow + Christians," I'd met Angela, a native Texan working for Campus Crusade for Christ in Moscow, and after a few

1. This means exactly what it says: we were a club of second graders who liked to look up pictures of birds in the encyclopedia.

emails, she'd agreed to be my Russian contact[2] on the trip. She'd even graciously written directions from the airport to our hotel. Our only problem, she warned, would be the Russian alphabet, which uses a combination of English letters, Greek letters, and drawings of spiders. On the Moscow metro, we were reduced to matching letters to find our stop, but to someone without advanced degrees in Russian linguistics, many of the stops looked similar, so it required a little more concentration than I was used to on public transit.[3] But after an hour of switching trains and fighting our way through impossibly crowded metro stations, we checked in to our hotel, located in the 1980 Olympic Village, the Olympics we boycotted (the United States, not Ryan and me). Thirty-two years later, the Olympic rings are still etched into the hotel's driveway.

For dinner we walked to a little shopping mall down the street, in part because we figured it would have a food court, but mostly because Air France had lost my luggage, and though Ryan said I could borrow some of his clothes, he was drawing the line at boxer shorts. Thankfully, the mall had underwear and a food court. They even had a KFC, though I couldn't figure out exactly how to order there and, while I tried, Russians kept jumping in front of me to place their orders. So I walked next door to the restaurant no one was eating at and pointed to a picture on the menu, and soon I was slurping what I believe was cabbage and onion soup. It tasted exactly like you'd imagine.

I did not enjoy my first day in Russia. I thought the people looked mean, and the food tasted meaner. But looking back, I realize my preconceived notions of the Russian people played a large part in shaping my experience. I lived through the last decade of the Cold War. I wasn't old enough to understand it, but I was old enough to fear the Russian nukes that could rain down on my parents' house at any moment. Mishka, a young man we met at church later in the week, told us his grandfather, a soldier in the Soviet Army, would tell him horror stories about the United States.

---

2. My Russian contact! How *Mission: Impossible* is that?

3. On a late night metro ride later in the week, a drunk man stumbled into our carriage and began punching the metro map on the wall. I could totally relate.

"When I was a boy, I remember inwardly celebrating the attacks on 9/11. I was glad America finally got what it deserved."

It gave me pause to hear someone say that, but would I have reacted any differently in fourth grade had something similar happened in Moscow? As far as evil goes, I had once believed the Russians were on a par with Darth Vader. Mishka said it wasn't until high school when a history professor kept driving home the fact that the Americans killed on 9/11 were simple people just like him that his opinions began to change. Now he is applying to graduate schools in the United States, while I still struggle not to view Russians through a Cold War lens. It was a quick and easy lesson in not judging an entire people by their leaders.

The next morning, we walked back to our metro stop, the unutterable Партизанская station. The Moscow metro is incredibly busy, moving more than seven million people on a weekday, but the stations are so beautiful the crowds don't bother you that much. Breathtaking mosaics, reflective marble walls, and massive chandeliers almost fool you into thinking you're strolling through a Parisian museum, until a train comes rumbling through. Our station had a massive statue in its terminal depicting Russian partisans resisting the Nazis in World War II. I found the scarf-headed old woman carrying an assault rifle to be particularly lifelike. After admiring the art, we wedged ourselves onto the next crowded train and hopped off in central Moscow, our first stop Red Square.

I'd been told that for pure tourism, St. Petersburg is a better choice than Moscow, and that may be so. All of the things you think you'd like to see when you visit Moscow—the Kremlin, Lenin's Tomb, St. Basil's, and the Kazan Cathedral—can be seen by standing in the center of Red Square and turning 360 degrees. That said, it's still quite a view.

Your eyes, assuming you're not color blind, are immediately drawn to St. Basil's Cathedral. It's probably what you think of when you think of Russia. In fact it's probably what you think of when you think of the Kremlin, because when you Google-search images of the Kremlin, almost half the photos are actually of St. Basil's.

Completed in 1561, the Cathedral of the Protection of Most Holy Theotokos on the Moat,[4] also known as the Cathedral of St. Vasily the Blessed (anglicized to St. Basil's), marks the geometric center of Moscow. Shaped like a bonfire's flames rising into the sky, nine vividly colored, onion-shaped domes surround the tallest golden dome in the center. During the Soviet Union's antitheist campaign (more on that in a bit), St. Basil's was confiscated from the Russian Orthodox Church and secularized in 1929. Today it remains the property of the Russian Federation.

Ryan and I stood in front of St. Basil's for a few minutes and just looked at it. I've seen old churches before—we'd seen Notre Dame just days earlier during our luggage-losing layover—but this place competes with Sagrada Familía in Barcelona as the most jaw-dropping church I've ever laid eyes on. Gawking complete, we bought tickets from the scowling woman in the booth next door and walked inside. It's a peculiar space, at least to me. Missing is the long nave with marble columns soaring into the heavens. It's not a great space that at once demonstrates the enormity of God and the smallness of you. Instead St. Basil's feels like a never-ending maze of small rooms and sanctuaries. It took us ten minutes to figure out how to leave the entrance area. In one of the larger sanctuaries, a men's quartet stood performing traditional Russian hymns, their voices rising up the cylindrical walls to the distant ceiling. When their song was finished, Ryan walked over and placed some rubles in their collection jar. The quartet thanked him by scolding him for wearing a hat indoors.

We skipped Lenin's Tomb because—actually, I don't have to give you a reason for not standing in a three-hour line to look at an embalmed Communist. Then after a tasty fried steak at Столовая 57, which slightly restored our faith in Russian cuisine, we took a stroll through GUM, one of the most expensive malls in the world.[5] GUM

4. I looked this up so you don't have to. Theotokos is the Greek name referring to the Virgin Mary, though I'm still not sure what it has to do with a moat.

5. We'd been told GUM was the most expensive mall in the world, and to test this claim, we priced a LaCoste polo shirt. The tag read py65060, which is around $165, so yeah, it's an expensive mall.

is an abbreviation of Glavnyi Universalnyi Magazin, which translates literally to "Main Universal Store," and I can attest that you can probably buy anything in the universe here. Inside GUM, below its vaulted glass ceiling, are endless galleries of high-end shopping, stacked three-stories high. Ryan and I stood on a glass bridge spanning one gallery to the next, both of us agreeing we didn't have enough money to be here and that we probably should leave before someone asked us to.

After GUM, we left Red Square through the Resurrection Gate, which was destroyed by Joseph Stalin in 1931, in part to continue his campaign to rid Russia of churches and holy relics, but also to make it easier to parade intercontinental missiles through the square.

At this point we had time to kill, and I suggested walking down to the river and taking a boat ride. Ryan disagreed, but I'd paid for our flights, so I won. Besides, Tricia and I had taken a river tour down the Seine in Paris and had a lovely time. Why wouldn't a ride down the Moskva be just as nice?

We paid our rubles and waited by the water until a boat arrived. The young Russian standing on the gangway became agitated when we handed him our tickets, pointing up the river and saying things we did not understand. We shrugged, and he shrugged, then he stamped our tickets and let us on board. We sat in the back of the boat on some plastic lawn chairs that were distributed indiscriminately across the deck, because two women with do-it-yourself haircuts had the only seats up front. And as much as I'd like to tell you the cool breezes and scenic views were worth the rubles, the techno music blaring from the boat's cabin made us strongly consider jumping overboard and swimming to shore.

Twenty long minutes later, we stopped and the haircut girls got off the boat while a few others got on. I noticed the captain talking to the young man who'd taken our tickets, both glancing in our direction after every sentence. Then the captain walked over to us and said, "Ticket." We handed him our tickets and he scrutinized them for a few seconds, then he looked up and said, "Finished!" Ryan and I looked at each other, then back to the captain who pointed to the exit and said,

"Off. Finished!" So we got off the boat, in the middle of who knows where, and began what turned out to be a ninety-minute walk back to Red Square, which included an eighty-minute lecture from Ryan on why the boat ride was a bad idea.

Back at Red Square, we rested our feet and people-watched until 5:00 p.m., when we walked toward the Church of Sts. Cosmas and Damian, a Russian Orthodox Church Angela suggested we visit. We arrived a little early and sat outside on a bench next to a statue of Vladimir Lenin sitting in a chair, his right arm draped over the chair's back, his left holding a book (probably *The Hunger Games*).

It was odd sitting between a church and a statue of Lenin, the first premier of the Soviet Union and the man who'd said all religion is used for "the exploitation and the stupefaction of the working class." The Soviet Union aimed to eliminate religion and replace it with universal atheism. In the months after the revolution, the state confiscated all church property, including the church buildings, and from 1922 to 1926, twenty-eight Russian Orthodox bishops and more than one thousand priests were killed. Persecution reached its height during the Great Purge of 1937–38, during which an estimated one hundred thousand priests were shot.

However, the right to believe was never officially outlawed, and believers were generally free to worship in private or at their churches, but public displays of religion were prohibited, as was the promotion of religion in mass media. This makes sense, as the vast majority of Russians at the time of the revolution were religious believers. The elimination of religion was a long-term goal of the Soviet Union, a battle they fought in the media[6] and in the schools. This explains why so many historic churches, such as St. Basil's, are still standing in Russia. Had the Soviets destroyed every church in the country and banned all

6. Take, for instance, Yuri Gagarin, the first human to fly to outer space. It was reported that during the flight, Gagarin said, "I don't see any God up here." However, these words do not appear in the verbatim flight transcripts. In fact Gargarin had been baptized into the Orthodox Church as a child and had his eldest daughter baptized just before his flight. The quote is said to have come from a Nikita Khrushchev speech during one of the state's antireligion campaigns.

religion, it likely would have resulted in another revolution. Instead they tolerated religion to a degree, fought it slowly, and at times even revived it for their own purposes, as Joseph Stalin did during World War II in an effort to intensify patriotic support for the war.

Ryan and I watched as a handful of people entered the church, waited a few minutes more, and then followed suit. We entered the side of the church, walking down a wide hallway where what I suspect were announcements were pinned on a large corkboard. Then turning left, we entered the nave, whose beautiful arched ceilings and colorful Byzantine icons momentarily distracted us from the fact that there was nowhere to sit, at least no pews, because in the Russian Orthodox Church, worshipers stand for nearly the entire service.

The Russian Orthodox Church is an Eastern Orthodox Church under the jurisdiction of the Patriarch of Moscow, a fellow by the name of Kirill I. With an estimated 225 to 300 million adherents worldwide, the Eastern Orthodox Church is the second largest church in the world, behind only the Roman Catholic Church. In the Eastern Orthodox Church, worship is understood to be work, and sitting is a form of rest, which explains the lack of pews. There were, however, a handful of benches along the outer wall of the worship space, so Ryan and I took a seat and waited for the service to begin.

More and more worshipers entered, making the sign of the cross as they did. We noticed one young man come in, light a candle in front of an icon, and begin praying, kneeling, standing, crossing himself, and, in a cool mixture of tradition and technology, occasionally pulling out his iPhone to read from a prayer book.

Ryan and I sat back watching all of this, whispering back and forth, both of us feeling an anxiety we couldn't quite articulate.

"Do you think we'll know what to do when the service starts?" I asked.

Ryan, who lived in New Orleans for a few years, was confident. "Yeah, I think so. It's probably like going to Mass, if we just—"

Out of nowhere the bearded priest, his robe flowing behind him, grabbed Ryan by the shoulder. We both stood up, apologizing for whatever it was we'd done, but the priest cut us off, speaking in agitated Russian, occasionally spitting out the word English. Ryan and I shrugged, and he held up a hand telling us to stay there. Seconds later, the priest and an older man came back to us, and the older man spoke in broken English, but we had no idea what he was saying, so he finally sat on the bench, crossed one leg over another, pointed at his legs, then shook a scolding finger in our direction. We apologized profusely, and as the two men walked away, we sat back down, with uncrossed legs.

The service began and the seventy-five or so in attendance gathered in the middle of the nave. We joined them, standing in the very back, trying as hard as we could not to be noticed again. At times people bowed and touched their fingers to the ground, and by the time we joined them, they were standing again. Ahead of us we could see the iconostasis, or wall of icons, behind which was the altar, where the priest and deacons were performing sacred rites. There was singing, and then the priest came through the left door of the wall, swinging an incense burner, followed by another man carrying a gold cross. The congregation moved in closer together, and the two men slowly circled the nave.

It's funny how the mind can calculate space and distance so easily. I knew in an instant there was not going to be enough room for the priest and his smoking ball of smell to pass between us and the back wall, but I was frozen, feet stuck to the floor. I just stared at the priest, who kept getting closer and closer, until finally his eyes bulged and with an angry hand he motioned for us to get out of his way.

I wanted the earth to open up and swallow us whole. Ten minutes in this church and I'd experienced more awkwardness than I could take. The room now smelled of strong incense, and I began to feel dizzy. I looked at Ryan and he also looked ill. He leaned over and asked if we could leave, but I thought he might vomit, and I knew that would make a great story for the book, so I said no. He was too sick to argue, but the rest of the service went off without incident, and as the congregation was dismissed, we slipped out into the fresh Moscow air. We did not fill out a visitors card.

As we quickly walked away from the Church of Sts. Cosmas and Damian, it was hard for me not to think of Russian Orthodoxy as some fringe denomination with strange rituals and an overly harsh stance on leg crossing. I think of the churches back home as the norm in Christianity, and everything else—well, I don't think of them much at all. But there are only sixteen million Southern Baptists in the world, and there are only twelve million United Methodists, and there are only around 350,000 PCA Presbyterians. Add them all together and they equal about one-fifth of the Russian Orthodox adherents worldwide. Look, I'm not saying we should all convert; I'm just saying we make up a very small part of Christianity, and while there are things other denominations can learn from us, there are also things we can learn from them. And now when I'm sitting through a sermon on a nice padded pew, I think of the 150,000,000 Russian Orthodox members worldwide who stand, because for them, worship is not a time of rest.

■ ■ ■

That evening[7] Ryan and I walked down the road from our hotel toward what looked like a putt-putt golf course for giants. This was the Izmailovo Kremlin, named for the Izmailovo district we were in, and it is part wedding complex, part flea market, because what girl doesn't dream of getting married in a Russian flea market? The brightly colored Byzantine-style buildings are modeled after Russian citadels, but unlike most citadels, ten kids with hammers could destroy this one in less than an hour. Ryan and I paid the small fee to enter the flea market and were overwhelmed by the selection. Where else on earth can you choose from nesting dolls, bearskin rugs, fur hats, framed portraits of Vladimir Lenin, DVDs of American films that have been in theaters only a few days, a variety of T-shirts featuring AK-47s, patent leather shoes, and just about anything else in the world you could possibly imagine, only dirtier? Ryan picked up a 1980 Moscow Olympics

---

7. It doesn't really get dark in Russia in June. The sun sets after ten, but the sky remains fairly bright until the sun rises around 4:45. Twilight golf rates are an excellent deal in this part of the world.

T-shirt, while I opted for an Auburn Cam Newton nesting doll, reluctantly passing on the fur hat, a decision I regret more with each passing day.

The next morning, we took the metro south to Akademicheskaya Station and met Angela and her roommate Jessica. Walking out of the station, we recounted our experience with Russian Orthodoxy and Angela just laughed. "Russians are always looking for something to get on you for," she said. "Don't worry about it."

On our walk, I confessed to Angela that my knowledge of Russian culture began and ended with *Rocky IV*. "I did read *Crime and Punishment* before the trip," I said, "but I'm not sure how much I understood. What's up with every Russian having four names? It's confusing."

Angela explained that Russians have a first name, then a patronymic middle name, followed by a family name. Since my dad's name is Alan, in Russia I would have been called Chad Alanavich Gibbs. The other problem is Russian first names have diminutives, so someone named Vladimir is also called Vova, and someone named Alexandra is also called Sasha. I'm not sure what the diminutive for Chad is, but I really hope it's Lando.

After a short walk, we arrived at Moscow Bible Church, which met in a large office building in south Moscow where many other churches meet throughout the day. We were upstairs in the largest space, but when I walked downstairs, I noticed other congregations of different races and nationalities meeting in smaller rooms. It felt like heaven, except all the denominations were being kept in separate rooms, so it felt like heaven if people were in charge.

Church that morning was about 97 percent less awkward than the day before. There were folding chairs to sit on, and legs could be crossed without concern. They even had donuts, coffee, and tea, though unlike back home, here the tea was black, not sweet.

Angela introduced us to Constantin, also known as Costya, director of Moscow Community Ministries of Campus Crusade for Christ Russia. Costya was born and raised in Russia but attended seminary in California, then spent a few years working at a church in Kentucky, which is why his English is better than mine, and why he has the only car in Moscow with a Kentucky Wildcats sticker on the bumper.

Standing in the back of the room while more and more worshipers filed in, Ryan and I recounted our Orthodox adventure, and Costya laughed. "That is actually one of the more progressive Orthodox Churches in Moscow." I said a quick prayer thanking God that Angela hadn't sent us to one of the more conservative ones.

I asked Costya about his time in America and what he saw in the church there. He told me a friend of his says when Christianity came to Greece, it became philosophy, and when it came to Europe, it became culture, and when it came to the United States, it became business. "That is a strength," he said, "because you have a very professional attitude toward worship, toward printing Bibles and other Christian literature. And I think that's what makes the US churches trendsetters for the rest of the world. When I go to church in the States, it's like seeing the future. You go to church and you know, okay, this will be happening around the globe in ten years."

"What are the challenges facing Christianity here?" I asked.

"The heritage of the Soviet Union is something that shouldn't be underestimated in terms of the horrible effect it had on male leadership. Under Communism, you were basically told you couldn't show any signs of leadership, you cannot show any signs of initiative. And as a result, men are very passive. So not only do you have to train men, you have to change their mentality."

But Costya is optimistic about the future of the church in what he refers to as post post-Christian Russia. "Russians are open to the mystical, to things we don't understand. Post-Christian society was very materialistic and had a negative aftertaste from their experiences with the church. The new generation doesn't have that aftertaste, and they are open to spiritual things."

We went on to talk about how generation X moved toward a hipper church, a pop church, but how the next generation, in America and in Russia, seems drawn to a more liturgical style of worship and doesn't mind if their church actually looks like a church. This may be a good thing, since there are many old church buildings available in European city centers. In Russia, belief in God appears to be growing. Nearly 75 percent of the country now identifies themselves as Russian Orthodox, almost double the percentage from twenty years ago at the fall of the Soviet Union. Protestants still make up only about 1 percent of the population, and only about 3 percent of Russians attend church two or three times a month, most going once a year or never. So it doesn't look like Russia is in the middle of some spiritual awakening, but even so, when you talk to someone like Costya, it's hard not to be excited about what the future may hold.

As the service began, we were given headsets to listen to the sermon translated into English, but first a couple of guitarists took the stage and led us in worship. The tunes were familiar, even if the words were not, and I hummed along as the congregation sang "As the Deer" in Russian.

The sermon that morning used chess illustrations, which is sort of like pastors in the South using college football references, and after the service, we did something very American; we all loaded up and went to a mall food court for lunch. Angela told me it was tradition and that many young people from church would sit in the food court for hours on Sunday fellowshiping.

Taking Angela's advice, I passed on McDonald's and ordered a plate of Russian dumplings, which tasted like my grandmother's dumplings, only more Russian, I suppose. I sat across the table from Dima, who grew up in Moldova and played college basketball in Russia. We talked sports for a while, and eventually the conversation turned to movies. I asked if he'd seen *Rocky IV*, and he laughed. I told him how Russians were generally portrayed in American films and asked how Americans were portrayed in Russian films. Dima hesitated, then said, "I don't want to offend you, but Americans are often portrayed as very wealthy … and very stupid."

Another group from the church asked Ryan where we were from in the States.

"Alabama," he said.

"Sweet home Alabama?" they replied, laughing.

"Yes, sweet home Alabama." Seems Lynyrd Skynyrd had beaten us to Moscow.

That afternoon we went to Gorky Park, which means Ryan whistled "Wind of Change" by the Scorpions all freaking day: *I follow the Moskva down to Gorky Park, listening to the wind of change.*

When you ride around on the Moscow metro, you get the impression that Russians are cold, unsmiling, emotionless people. Granted, Russians are different from Americans. In Alabama you can turn to the person behind you in line at Walmart and say, "My name's Chad. Where do you go to church and who did you vote for in the last election?" and no one would think strangely of you. Try that in Russia and the person will slowly back away, assuming that you'd somehow escaped from the asylum. That said, maybe it's best not to judge a people by the way they act on public transportation. Go see how they act in a park.

In Gorky Park the weather was brilliant and there were smiling, laughing people everywhere. Folks were riding bikes, rollerblading, and skateboarding. Parents were chasing kids and couples were lying on blankets in the grass. We laughed as Russian girls posed for photographs next to an old piano. And by posing, I mean supermodel posing. "Russian girls are taught to pose like that from birth," Angela said. "They make fun of me for not doing it."

Then later that day, we toured the Moscow Kremlin, which I'd always sort of pictured as the Russian version of the White House. It is, in a sense, but it's also much more. Inside the fortified complex, whose walls were built in the fifteenth century, are four cathedrals and five palaces, including the Kremlin Senate, which houses the presidential administration, although the president actually lives at an estate called Novo-Ogaryovo in west Moscow.

Ryan and I toured the cathedrals, gawked at the thirty-nine-ton Tsar Cannon, then found a vendor selling ice cream. It was strange, sitting on a bench in the Kremlin, eating chocolate ice cream. I remembered the way I thought about Russia and Russians back in our second grade bird club, and this was not a day I could have foreseen. But now I have Russian friends. Costya and I chat on Skype, and Dima and I wish each other happy birthday on Facebook. And now when I think of Russia, I think of them, not nuclear weapons raining down on my elementary school. Maybe Rocky was right. Everybody can change. Even me.

UGANDA

I bless the rains down in Africa.

—Toto, "Africa"

Who's the oldest person you've made cry?" I asked the nurse holding a tray of needles. She was my first sign that visiting Africa is a little different from, say, visiting Florida. The nurse flashed a demented smile, turning slightly so I could see the tattoo on her neck that read, "Your pain is my pleasure," and said, "Hopefully, you'll be it." Then she proceeded to jab me with needle after needle, protecting me from hepatitis A, hepatitis B, typhoid fever, tetanus, pertussis, mad cow disease, mad zombie disease, jungle worms, electric flu, purple tooth syndrome, hangnails, kryptonite, the common cold, and acne. I didn't cry, but I didn't really like it either.

Then the doctor came in, asked about my trip, and scribbled a prescription for malaria pills. "These," he said, holding up the prescription, "are known to cause vivid dreams or night terrors."

"Wait, doc, do they cause vivid dreams *or* night terrors? Because there is a big difference between riding a unicorn around Fenway Park and being eaten by a unicorn at Fenway Park."

The doctor just smiled and said, "Side effects may vary."

■ ■ ■

When I fly, I often wonder about the other passengers on my flight. I wonder what their stories are and why they're going wherever it is we're all going. Sometimes I make up stories about them and am disappointed when the man next to me unzips his carry-on to reveal a laptop, and not a human head and three hundred thousand dollars in unmarked bills. But I don't think I've ever been more intrigued about my flight mates than on our KLM flight from Amsterdam to Entebbe, Uganda. After we'd all eaten our vacuum-sealed chicken, I wanted to stand up and say, "Hi, my name is Chad. Why don't we go around the plane and each of us share why exactly we're going to Uganda?"

There were people in business suits and people dressed for safari, and judging by T-shirts and overheard conversations, many of the passengers were on some sort of missions trip. Tricia and I were traveling with Jonathan Savage and Pat Bethea, the director of missions strategy and the newly hired youth pastor of Cornerstone Church, our church in Auburn. We were going to Uganda to visit the leaders of Buloba Community Church, a church Cornerstone has partnered with since 2007, and to meet with local physicians to discuss the logistics of running a health clinic in Buloba sometime in 2013. Actually, that's what Tricia, Jonathan, and Pat were doing; my job was to stay out of their way.

As our plane crossed the equator, I flipped through a Ugandan guidebook I'd picked up the week before. More than 85 percent of Ugandans identify themselves as Christian, around half Catholic, half Protestant.[1] Missionaries have been coming here since the late nineteenth century, even before Uganda was incorporated into the British Empire. Because of the British, English is still the official language of Uganda, though most Ugandans also speak Luganda or Swahili or one of forty other local dialects.

Before our trip, I chatted with Godfrey, a native Ugandan and a friend of a friend, and he told me that even before the missionaries, "Ugandans had their cultural way of understanding and relating to a god. They were worshipers, but they were worshiping what they did not understand. Unfortunately, I would say the missionaries did not break through the worldviews of the Africans when they presented the gospel. It was like they found someone wearing a coat, and they gave them another coat to put on top and feel warmer. So in Uganda today, it is common to find someone very devoted in church, but at the same time devoted to their traditional animistic beliefs. There is a lot of syncretism in Uganda."

After a short stopover in Rwanda, we flew to Entebbe International Airport on Lake Victoria, the same airport made famous in 1976 when the Popular Front for the Liberation of Palestine hijacked an Air France A300 and held more than one hundred passengers, mostly Israelis, hostage for one week.

Since gaining its independence in 1961, Uganda has been one of the world's most war-torn countries. This is thanks in no small part

1. Muslims make up around 12 percent of the Ugandan population.

to Idi Amin, an insane man who ran the country for most of the seventies. In recent years, things have been I guess what you'd call stable. Stable enough that I wasn't that concerned about taking my wife there. But even so, it's worth noting that the current administration came to power in a bloody 1986 coup and spent years fighting a civil war against the Lord's Resistance Army, led by Joseph Kony, a fellow you may have seen on YouTube.

We landed, without international incident, around 10:00 p.m. local time. Ours was the only flight into Kampala that hour, so the line through immigration moved swiftly. The only thing about the process that struck me as odd was the entry visa, which was acquired not by mailing your passport to an embassy weeks in advance but by handing a man fifty dollars at the airport. I'm not sure the visa program is designed to make sure the Ugandan government knows everyone who is entering the country so much as to make sure everyone who enters the country pays the Ugandan government fifty dollars.

In the lobby, Jonathan bought us all the greenest Mountain Dews I'd ever seen. We drank them, hesitantly, all of us wondering whether the vaccines we'd received protected us from whatever it was making the soda glow. Then we walked outside into the dimly lit parking lot to meet Patrick Sserunjogi (pronounced Pa-TRICK), president of Bridge Africa International.[2]

I did not enjoy the forty-five minute drive from Entebbe Airport to the capital city of Kampala, because I do not enjoy the sensation of imminent fiery death. Okay, that's not entirely fair. We never came close to dying. It's just that Ugandans drive a little differently than we do. Not better or worse, just different. The van probably never exceeded forty miles per hour, but to me it felt like weaving through the Macy's Thanksgiving Day Parade at forty miles per hour.

The choreography of it all is actually quite amazing. On a busy two-lane road, cars are driving in both directions at vastly different speeds.

---

2. Bridge Africa is an organization that, well, bridges others to Africa. While we were in Uganda, Patrick and his staff fed us, housed us, transported us, and basically kept us from doing anything stupid.

We'd come up behind a slow-moving car and Patrick would flash his lights or honk his horn or turn on a blinker, and all of a sudden we would be heading straight toward oncoming traffic. How fast Patrick would pass was determined by how fast the oncoming car was moving. Sometimes we got back into our lane seconds before a crash, but we always got back over, usually because the car we'd passed would slow up and let us in. This seemed to work only because, unlike back home, drivers in Uganda are very attentive. They have to be. If texting and driving ever catches on in Kampala, I'm not going back.

It was close to midnight, but people were out everywhere on the Kampala-Entebbe Road. Markets, restaurants, and barrooms all looked busy, and the road was full of cars and vans, motorcycles zipping between them. A man stumbled into the road, and Patrick swerved to miss him, laughing, then saying in his clipped, conjunction-free English, "I believe that man has had too much to drink tonight."

We finally made it to the Green Valley Hotel on Ggaba Road around midnight. Pulling up to the unmanned gate, Patrick honked his horn like he was being paid by the honk. This went on for at least a minute, until everyone in south Kampala was awake and an angry guard came walking up the driveway. Patrick turned to us and said, "I hope this man does not have a gun." We all laughed, not sure whether he was joking.

The man did have a gun, but he didn't use it on us, and soon Tricia and I were in our room, where we brushed our teeth with bottled water, then fell asleep without realizing that the contraption over our bed was the mosquito net and we probably should lower it. Thankfully, the Ugandan mosquitoes didn't find us tasty.

The next morning, we ate breakfast at the hotel in a small courtyard overlooking lush green mountains. Eggs and fruit were on the menu, and as far as we could tell, we were the only guests at the hotel. To oblige us, the hotel staff rolled out a small television and turned it to E!, which I assume is what they think Americans like to watch in the morning.[3]

---

3. In the evenings, the hotel played old country music over loudspeakers in the garden, ensuring that forevermore when I hear "Islands in the Stream," I will think of Uganda.

When our server brought out orange juice, Jonathan asked if we could have some coffee. "Drinking coffee?" she replied, leading all of us to believe our hotel served some sort of eating coffee, but none of us was brave enough to ask for it during our stay.

After breakfast we loaded up the van and journeyed east to Buloba, a thirty-minute drive from Kampala. "Closer to an hour," Patrick said, "before the road was improved." Progress!

We took the Northern Bypass, a new, modern highway skirting the edge of Kampala, and where the bypass meets the Mityana Road that takes you toward Buloba sits a roundabout designed, undoubtedly, by a civil engineer who tortured animals as a child. It was a whirling mass of speeding, honking cars and vans, intersected in all directions by streaking motorcycles. If I'd been driving, I'd have pulled over to the side of the road and cried. However, Patrick calmly navigated his way through, even pointing out the terrifying marabou storks (aka undertaker birds) gathered on the roadside.

We turned off the Mityana Road about a mile past the God Is Love Pork Joint and arrived at Buloba Community Church as children at the Ebenezer School were lining up for lunch next door. The church runs the school in partnership with Africa Renewal Ministries' (ARM) Child Development Project.[4] Members of Cornerstone Church in Auburn sponsor more than three hundred children in Buloba through ARM, providing them with a meal a day, uniforms, health care, and education.

Walking through the dusty Ebenezer schoolyard toward the church, we noticed dozens of African children with shaved heads hiding in doorways, whispering and giggling as we passed. I heard the word *mzungu* for the first time, though certainly not for the last.

Mzungu is a Swahili word for "someone who roams around aimlessly," which didn't really fit us, since we had a guide and all. But I believe the kids' usage, along with the countless other times we heard the word during our stay, translated closer to, "Hey, look—white people!"

---

4. *www.africarenewalministries.org.*

We entered the church, a large brick structure with open windows and a dirt-covered concrete floor, and found Pastor Eva, lead pastor of Buloba Community, and some of the other staff sitting around a table working on laptops. Jonathan made introductions, and I wandered around the sanctuary taking photographs. Again I noticed four or five kids peeking around the doorway and giggling, then I saw more of them in the windows.

I motioned to Pat and the two of us walked outside, and within seconds, they were on us like the walking dead, but instead of eating us, they were grabbing our hands, hugging our legs, and constantly pulling at the hair on our arms. "How are you, mzungu?" they asked us over and over again. I felt like a celebrity, or more likely a character at Disney World. More kids came running, and soon Pat and I were enclosed in a giant circle of laughing African schoolchildren, all wanting to pull the hair on our arms.

"What is your name?" one of them asked me, and I said, "Chad."

"Chad!" they all yelled, then laughed even more. Soon they were running around, pointing and calling each other Chad. I had a creeping suspicion second graders were mocking me. When I told adults my name, they always said, "Chad, like the country! You must be African. Ha ha ha ha!" I had a creeping suspicion they were mocking me as well.

It's tradition for groups from Cornerstone to fetch water for the school on their first visit to Buloba, so Pastor Eva and two associate pastors led us downhill through a mile-long jungle trail to the freshwater well. I walked next to one of the associate pastors, a young man in his twenties, who insisted on holding my hand while discussing his anger that President Obama had legalized gay marriage. I told him the president only said that he supports gay marriage, then I tried, and failed, to explain our branches of government and separation of powers.

If you've caught a news story out of Uganda lately, you know that homosexuality is, to put it mildly, frowned upon there, and on this trip I spoke to more than one Ugandan who lamented America's slide into gayness. However, even American Christians who share the Ugandan view on same-sex relationships would probably think the African nation has gone a little too far with its Anti-Homosexuality Act, since gay men and women are subject to life in prison under the law. This actually is better than the original bill, though, which called for homosexuals to face the death penalty.

Down at the well, the pastors filled up what I recall were two five-hundred-gallon jugs, then Pat, Jonathan, and I took turns lugging them back up to the church. The handles on the jugs cut deep into our hands, and every fifty yards or so, we set them down and switched hands. I was dripping with sweat and complaining bitterly in my head when two kids smaller than the jugs we were carrying darted past us up the hill, both carrying large jugs of their own. Then I had some guilt to carry up the hill with the water.

While we were carrying the water back to the church, one of the pastors used his cell phone, and it struck me we were in a place where you had to walk a mile for fresh water, yet you could tweet, using a small computer you carry in your pocket, a photo of yourself carrying the water. In some ways, the twenty-first century has beaten the twentieth century to Uganda.

Before we left to go back to Kampala, Tricia and I asked Pastor Eva about meeting our sponsored child. We, like so many members of our church, give a few dollars each month through ARM to support a child in Buloba. Our sponsored child is an eight-year-old girl named Linet, and Pastor Eva said of course we could meet her, and that she lived "just up the road." Just up the road in Uganda apparently means a thirty-minute trek through the jungle, but eventually we were standing in front of a small, terrified little girl who kept looking down at her feet. We introduced ourselves, and without looking up, she whispered in the tiniest of voices, "Linet."

"We terrified her," Tricia said on our drive back to Kampala.

And we did, a little. Though I suppose if a couple of Africans had shown up at Glencoe Elementary School when I was eight years old and started hugging me and taking pictures with me and talking Swahili to me, I'd have been a little scared myself. In retrospect, it's amazing Linet didn't scream and run into the jungle. But she warmed up to us a little more on each successive visit to Buloba, and on our last day in Uganda, we spent an hour at her home, meeting her brothers and sisters and cousins and talking to her grandmother through an interpreter.

Believe me, Tricia and I are under no delusions that we are saving Africa by donating thirty-five bucks each month, but sponsoring Linet, and writing her letters and receiving letters from her, has been incredibly rewarding, and I do think we're making her life a little better. Sure, you can probably find an article online suggesting these child sponsorship programs are a bad thing, but you can also find articles online suggesting that breathing oxygen is a bad thing. There are fantastic child sponsorship programs operating across the globe, and having seen some of their work firsthand, I hope you will check them out. And if you ever get the opportunity to meet your sponsored child, I hope you take it, because the hug Linet gave us as we left Buloba on our last day is a memory I will cherish forever.

By then we'd moved from the hotel to a house rented by Bridge Africa, and we had our first of many home-cooked Ugandan meals of fried chicken, Irish potatoes, avocados, matooke (steamed green bananas), chapatti bread, eggplant, beans, rice, peanut sauce, beef, carrots, green beans, and fish, though not all at once. To drink, we chose from bottled water, Coca-Cola, Diet Coke, Orange Fanta, and something called Stoney Tangawizi, a ginger beer I tried only once. And each night for dessert, we had pineapple so unbelievably sweet that Tricia still dreams about it.

■ ■ ■

A few days later, we were back in Buloba meeting with Pastor Eva and her staff, discussing Cornerstone's future relationship with the Ugandan church. We also discussed the freshwater well Cornerstone had paid for that sits a hundred yards behind the church—the broken one we'd walked past the day before on our way to the next well, a mile away. It would cost around six hundred dollars to fix, and I remember thinking Tricia and I could write a check for that right now. Maybe they'd even put our names on it. But then Pastor Eva spoke of the way the well had been abused by others in the community, and by some from outside the community. How men would come at night and make bricks from the dirt around the well. They told us no one was worried about breaking it, because they knew as soon as they did, more white people would come and fix it.

After our trip, I spoke to Brian Johnson, one of the pastors at Cornerstone, about this, and he told me, "We are stunting their growth with our 'save Africa' mentality." Tricia and I worry about this more after visiting Africa. We're more diligent researching the organizations we give to, hoping our gifts aren't hurting more than they help, because I fear sometimes that's what we are doing.

The well in Buloba is a good example, because I wanted to pay to fix it, and if the community abused it and it broke again, I'd probably want to pay to fix it again. I wanted to fix the well in part because I wanted to do something good, but also because I felt guilty. A sense of guilt pervaded a large part of my time in Uganda, because I witnessed poverty there unlike anything I'd seen before. Our dogs sleep in nicer conditions than the little girl we sponsor, and I'd have to be an incredibly callous person to see that and not be moved to do something. But moved to do what is the question, because trying to turn all of Uganda into a nice American suburb probably isn't the answer. I think guilt has its purposes, but oftentimes when we act out of guilt, we act only to rid ourselves of the guilty feelings. Paying to fix that well over and over again would make me feel better about having a PlayStation 3, but it surely wouldn't help the community in Buloba; it would only create long-term dependence and elevate me to a weird parent-savior role that, sadly, a depraved part of me does find appealing.

My Ugandan friend Godfrey agreed, saying, "Africans commonly want to carry themselves as always being needy, and people from the West often want to come in as saviors. This has negative implications, and the relationship between Africa and the West has become a dependency, not a partnership."

"Africa is poor," Godfrey continued, "but I think it is mostly a poverty of mindsets. God has endowed us with resources, but our unredeemed culture of corruption and selfishness holds us back. So people come from the West and see that we are poor and think all they can do is give us cash and clothes to improve our welfare. But I think we need more than welfare; we need to learn from one another, for the betterment of each other."

Godfrey works for New Hope Uganda, a children's center home to more than a hundred and fifty Ugandan orphans, so he's not discounting that humanitarian aid is sometimes vital, and that caring for others' physical needs is at the heart of the gospel. But there can be unintended consequences to our charity, like when sending thirty men halfway around the world to build a church puts local construction workers out of a job. And granted, I managed only a C-minus in my one economics course at Auburn, but people much smarter than me believe a constant stream of aid actually chokes local economies, keeping Africans poor. Ugandans have seen wasteful spending, and they've seen government corruption, and when I talk to some of them, I think, Okay, enough with the short-term missions projects where we fly teams of twenty men around the world to rebuild something we built two years earlier. And enough with the handouts that corrupt government officials skim off the top of. Ugandans need full-time missionaries to live among and disciple them. But then I hear another view.

"I know this will anger some American Christians, but I do not believe many of the full-time missionaries here do much good." This came from Omara,[5] another Ugandan I spoke with in Kampala. "They come here and live in houses that 99 percent of Ugandans cannot afford, they spend most of their time together drinking coffee at the same mall, and even though they do not mean to, they set themselves so far apart from the everyday Ugandan that I believe they become ineffectual."

In the course of writing this chapter, I wrote and deleted probably twenty sentences in this space. Most began with something like, "As Christians, we need to ..." Then I wrote some vague, Christiany

5. Omara is a pseudonym.

catchall solution to the problems of Uganda. But I spent only eight days in Uganda, and to pretend I even understand the country, let alone have any answers to its problems, would be ridiculous. But that's a trap so many of us fall into when we think about Africa only as a problem that needs to be solved. I set out to experience Christian culture around the world, and a large part of Christian culture in Uganda is the Western missionary presence. I've tried to present that here, along with some thoughts on what locals think may actually be hurting more than helping. But for a clearer picture, you are going to have to read a much smarter book than this one, or better yet, you should go and see Uganda for yourself.

■ ■ ■

On our way back to the hotel, we drove through downtown Kampala so Jonathan could stop at the Orange store[6] and inquire about mobile Wi-Fi. With gridlocked traffic and high-rise buildings, Kampala's downtown feels similar to any other downtown, only rawer, and with a lot more guns. Men with guns guard the shops, men with guns guard the parking lots, and men with guns guard men with guns. It was all a little unnerving.

We fought our way through traffic to a gated parking lot that was obviously reserved for people other than us, but Patrick spoke to the guard in Swahili, then handed him some shillings, then we parked. Afterward we went to a mall for food-court pizza, and I remember thinking Uganda, at least at times, was nothing like I'd thought it would be. My sister-in-law asked before we left if we'd be sleeping in huts, and while I didn't expect it to be that primitive, I didn't really expect to eat in a mall after shopping for mobile Wi-Fi. My high school friend Matt lives with his family in Uganda, and we joked about this. "I have to remind people we're not living in a 1975 issue of *National Geographic*," he said.

One morning after breakfast, we traveled to the Ggaba fish market,

6. Orange is a Paris-based telecommunications company. Like Apple, they do not sell fruit.

which smelled strongly of cinnamon (just kidding, it smelled strongly of fish), and we hired a boat to take us across Lake Victoria. Lake Victoria, named after Queen Victoria of England, is the largest lake in Africa and apparently is home to man-eating crocodiles. I did not know this as we skimmed across the water in a long, low, and leaky boat, so I'm smiling, not crying, in all the pictures we took.

From there we made our way to the Wentz Medical Center, a modern, two-story brick building in Ggaba that is part of ARM's Renewal Healthcare Network. We met with Martin, a doctor on staff, to discuss the logistics of running a clinic in Buloba, and while he and Tricia talked doctor talk, the rest of us nodded along. At one point Dr. Martin spoke of a clinic he'd run where an American nurse told a group of African women about having a miscarriage, and none of the women could believe it. "There are Ugandans who believe mzungus do not die," he said. "So it was good for them to hear this." And I can see where they would get this impression. We fly in with our piles of money, fix things, then fly away. We are like superheroes without capes.[7]

Godfrey told me, "Fear of death is a challenge for Ugandans. It affects how we respond to the gospel. Here it is quite common for people to claim they are saved, so long as they were promised to be alive or to be healed from some disease. Here when someone dies, especially a believer or a Christian leader, people's faith can be shaken tremendously."

This fear of death seems to be a byproduct of the health, wealth, and prosperity gospel that has found its way to Uganda. "Not necessarily through missionaries," Godfrey said, "but from watching American churches on television." Uganda is one of the poorest countries in the world, so counting on God to make you rich might seem like a long shot. But no one wants to die, and it's no new trend for crooked pastors to link a person's health to their spiritual life, particularly their financial giving. Can't you just hear a pastor saying, "Look at the westerners, they give generously and God has made them rich and healthy." If this

---

7. Yes, there are superheroes who don't wear capes, like Flash and Green Lantern, among others, but you know what I mean, you big nerd.

was the only "good news" you'd heard, of course the death of a seemingly faithful believer would shake your faith.

■ ■ ■

That evening after dinner, we lost power, not an uncommon occurrence in Kampala, so Tricia and I sat on the balcony upstairs and watched the sunset over the mountains. We heard the adhan, the Islamic call to prayer, from the mosque below as it competed with the megaphoned Christian pastor shouting from the back of his van. I enjoyed hearing those things in the evenings, but not so much at sunrise, when they battled the roosters to see who could wake us up first.

On Sunday, Eddie, an employee of Bridge Africa and Uganda's answer to Jeff Gordon, drove us to Ggaba Community Church, where Patrick, Dr. Martin, and many others we'd met worship on Sundays.

Inside, Ggaba Community Church looks like any other modern church back home. Large video screens are mounted above both sides of the stage, and lights and speakers hang from the ceiling. There were probably four hundred in attendance at our service, and another larger service took place after ours.

The morning sun was beaming through the balcony windows as we sang worship songs, most of them familiar to anyone who's been to church in the last ten years, then a group of four young people sang another song, then a guy I can only describe as the church's hype man took the stage and worked the place into a frenzy. He spoke—well, yelled—about Jesus telling his disciples they could move mountains with their faith, then he began shouting, "Mountain movers, rise up!" and soon the church was on its feet.

Many of the churches I visited for this book felt similar to churches back home, and it makes sense, since around the world people told me their churches are shaped by American Christian culture. I wasn't expecting this to be the case in Uganda, but only because I was so ignorant of Uganda. Sitting there on a wooden pew, I was reminded of what my friend Matt told me before my trip. He said, "A lot of people think they are 'bringing Christ to Africa.' Don't get me wrong, there are still unreached people groups, but specifically in Uganda, I can tell you that the gospel of Christ is alive and well. They are not a lost people any more than we are. As a matter of fact, being home on furlough, America is feeling every bit as spiritually dark to me, if not more so, than anywhere I've lived in Uganda." It's embarrassing to admit, but there was a naive part of me that thought of Ugandans as a bunch of worry free people sitting around the jungle waiting for westerners to come teach them Bible stories. But of course Ugandans' lives are as rich and complex as ours or anyone else's. Just spending a week around Patrick, I saw a perfect example of a man living out his faith and trying to provide a brighter future for his four children while wondering if the power will be on later that evening when Chelsea FC plays an exhibition match.

However, I have to remind myself that Ugandan culture can be very different from the culture I grew up in, even if we both sing Chris Tomlin songs at church. Jeff Atherstone is the vice chancellor of Africa Renewal University in Kampala, and he told me about a particular incident in his college for which I had no cultural reference.

"Tribalism and syncretism with traditional African religions can be a real challenge for Ugandans," Jeff said. "Recently I had a staff member get into a dispute with her department head. The staff member is a Muhima, which is the president's tribe, and her department head is an Eteso. In her tribe, she was taught as a Muhima she could never be wrong. That the Muhima were 'true humans' and superior to all other tribes. So even though she has a BA in theology and a master of divinity, when a dispute broke out, she could not admit she was wrong. More than ten staff witnessed the event and met with her one-on-one to calm her down and share that she was wrong. But ultimately she chose to leave her job rather than admit she was wrong."

We left the church in Ggaba after the sermon so we could make it out to Buloba Community Church for part of their Sunday morning service, and when we arrived, there were seats waiting for us up front. A cool breeze drifted through the open windows of the church, and the dust, kicked up by children and adults in colorful costumes performing traditional African dances to upbeat drum music, sparkled in the morning sun. There were a hundred and fifty or so people in attendance that morning, some families from the community, many children from the school, and one little boy who insisted on sitting in Pat Bethea's lap for the duration of the sermon, which was delivered by an associate pastor who was training at the Bible college up the road. I've been to some highly choreographed and flawlessly executed worship services, but this was not one of them. Speakers crackled, microphones malfunctioned, and children were brought in to perform, then ushered back outside because the right music could not be found. I can see how this might not fly back home, but here there was laughter and patience and a sense of "it's Sunday; where else do we have to be but in the house of the Lord?" In all, the service lasted about three hours, so I guess it goes without saying that we didn't beat the Baptists to lunch, but Jonathan brought Clif Bars, so after a while I stopped looking at my watch too, because I couldn't think of anywhere else I'd rather be.

■ ■ ■

On our final evening in Uganda, Patrick took us to a swanky restaurant on a mountain overlooking Lake Victoria. The night air felt incredible as we sat on an outdoor patio and watched the sun set behind the city. We reflected on the week while eating like lions, consuming absurd amounts of beef, pork, chicken, and any other dead animal set in front of us. It felt like the perfect end to an amazing trip, and to cap it off, sometime during dessert, Toto's "Africa" came on over the speakers, much to the delight of us four mzungus.

"When we first heard this song," Patrick said, "it made us all so proud to be African."

I think about this every time Toto plays during some eighties flashback lunch hour on my radio, and I think about how proud I am to say I now know Africans. And in lieu of some overly sappy close to this chapter, in which I make some sentimental statement about how visiting Uganda changed my life, I'll just say that I dream about the day I will get to go back there—on a man-eating unicorn. Stupid malaria pills.

ITALY

Three hearts in the fountain,
Each heart longing for its home.
There they lie in the fountain
Somewhere in the heart of Rome.
—Sammy Cahn, "Three Coins in the Fountain"

Buongiorno."

"What does that mean?" my mom asked.

"It means good morning," I said. "Try saying it."

"I can't."

"Just try."

"I'll just tell them good morning."

If you don't count a twenty-four-hour jaunt into Canada—and who does, eh?—neither of my parents had ever left the United States until October 2012, when I took them with me to Italy. Not wanting to hear that I had to check one of them into an Italian hospital, Tricia warned me repeatedly before the trip to pace myself. This is not because my parents are old (they're both in their midfifties), and it's not because they are in bad health (they are not). She warned me because while traveling, I tend to walk like a lunatic. I walk faster and farther than anyone with me wants to walk, and it's not until I lay down in the evening that I realize I've set the half-marathon record for racewalking. I promised Tricia we'd take things at a leisurely pace in Italy, but warned my folks they might want to start some sort of fitness regimen, just in case.

We spent a day in London before flying to Leonardo da Vinci–Fiumicino Airport and taking a taxi to our hotel near Villa Borghese. The forty-five-minute drive through Rome was lovely, even if the driver risked our lives by driving with a large map unfurled across his steering wheel. At one point, we passed a gaggle of nuns,[1] and I thought about the three of us, all Alabama Protestants, in the heart of Catholicism. Growing up in Glencoe, Alabama, I knew of one Catholic church in the area, and I don't think I knew even one Catholic kid, though I'd heard rumors they existed. I do remember hearing that Catholics drink, a lot. I heard that Catholics pray to Mary, not Jesus. And I heard Catholics believe they earn their way to heaven, and they don't even really believe that, because their religion is just a bunch of traditions that even they don't really care about. It wasn't until I lived in Mobile (which has a much higher percentage of Catholics than the rest of Alabama) that my thoughts and opinions on the Catholic

1. A group of nuns is called a gaggle, right? A murder of nuns?

Church evolved a little, but even so, the things you learn as a child can be hard to unlearn.

We made it to our room a little after noon, and while my parents napped, I called home to check on Tricia. I'm terribly annoying when away from home, calling multiple times a day to check on everything from our dogs to our 401(k). But this trip, I knew I'd be worse, because sometime between Uganda and now, Tricia and I had—how do I say this delicately?—begun the process of populating the earth.

"Yes, you woke me up, and yes, I am fine, and yes, I'm sure the baby is fine."

"Okay, I just wanted to check. So the ultrasound is on Monday?"

"Yes, and I told you I'd send pictures. Just try to enjoy Italy, okay? Now, what are your plans for tonight?"

"We'll probably just take it easy. Tomorrow is sightseeing, maybe go to Vatican City."

At this Tricia broke into parody song: "Everything's up-to-date in Vatican City. They've gone about as far as they can go."

Despite telling Tricia we'd take it easy, I decided we needed to see the sunset from atop Janiculum Hill, the second tallest hill in Rome. This involved riding the metro to the Circo Massimo Station, then taking a bit of a hike. Looking at Google Maps, I knew the walk was about a mile, as the crow flies, but unfortunately my parents are not crows, and our walk was closer to three miles (twelve miles when my dad tells the story), past the Circus Maximus, across the Ponte Palatino, then along the Tiber River before turning left and winding our way up the hill by the San Pietro in Montorio, where, according to tradition, St. Peter was crucified. We had to stop a few times to catch our breath, and each time, I could hear Tricia's scolding voice ringing in my ears, but we made it to the top without experiencing a traumatic cardiac event and even had a few glorious minutes of sunset to spare.

From atop Janiculum Hill, the domes and towers of the city that once ruled the world are laid out before you, basking in the setting sun. And if you grow weary of that view, simply walk around the Garibaldi statue and look behind you toward the giant dome of St. Peter's Basilica.

I think we would have stayed up there for hours, but Janiculum Hill is a bit of a make-out spot, and the public displays of affection were slowly turning into public displays of procreation, so we hailed a taxi and went in search of dinner.

That evening, I did not order wine with dinner because we committed what might be the unpardonable sin; we ate at McDonald's in Italy. But I didn't order wine the rest of the week either, a symptom of my Baptist teetotaling upbringing, and I've thought about that a lot since we returned. Growing up, the reason we were given to abstain from alcohol was that some lost person might see us drinking and be completely turned off by Christianity. Of course I understand telling children and teens to abstain, but telling adults to abstain, particularly when you insinuate that alcohol consumption is sinful, well, then we're getting into weird territory. Besides, I think hypothetical Lost Larry would actually be more likely to come to church with someone he saw having wine at dinner, but maybe that's just me.

Washing down my McNuggets with a warm Diet Coke, I recalled a conversation I had before the trip with Paula, a Catholic and a native Italian who now lives in the buckle of the American Bible Belt. I'd been introduced to Paula's daughter by a friend, and when I asked if her mother had some thoughts on the church in America, she said, "Oh, yeah, she'll have lots of thoughts on that." When I spoke to Paula, I'm not sure I'd even finished my first question when she began, "There's some stuff here, especially the Baptists, that I'm not crazy about. The fact that you're not supposed to drink or dance. My husband and I are not drinkers—we may drink a glass of wine a month—but all of the rules, you cannot do this, cannot do that. To tell you the truth, all the people I know who are Baptists, they're a bunch of liars."

If a denomination says wine is a blessing, people will call them drunks, and if a denomination says drinking wine is sinful, people will call them liars, and I don't suppose that will change anytime soon. Still, people say Catholics drink too much, and joke about Catholic guilt, yet when surrounded by Catholics drinking in moderation, I was the one afraid to order a glass of wine in front of my parents, who wouldn't have cared anyway. Besides, water in Italy costs €6; the wine would have been cheaper.

After McDinner we went to see the Colosseum, and while there are many different ways to get there, for me nothing beats riding the metro to the aptly named Colosseo stop, then walking up the stairs and out onto the street to be confronted by the massive ancient stadium just yards away. It's one of the most "holy cow, I'm in Italy" moments you can have.

Mom and I took a seat on a nearby bench while Dad began the slow process of photographing the old stadium from every possible angle.[2] Around us hundreds of tourists were being harassed by dozens of men selling everything from Colosseum models to these strange little glow-in-the-dark helicopters that you could launch nearly a hundred feet into the air and watch slowly glide down. Two of the guys selling helicopters approached us and began showing off their wares.

"No, thanks," we said seventeen or eighteen times, until one of them left, while the other just stood next to me, smiling.

"Where are you from?" I asked him, not knowing what else to say.

"I am from India," he replied.

"I'm traveling to India later this year," I told him. "Visiting New Delhi."

"You do not need to go to Delhi," he said and walked away. I hoped this wasn't some sort of prophetic foreshadowing.

Dad found us a few minutes later, I assume because his memory card was full, and the three of us walked around the Colosseum, turning down a side street to visit the same gelato shop where Tricia and I had first sampled the life-changing dessert two years earlier. This was the first of an estimated six thousand cones of gelato we consumed during the trip.

Saturday morning I tried to get Mom to greet our waiter with "buongiorno," but she refused, and instead my parents learned that

---

2. I'd be remiss if I didn't mention the terrifying moment when my dad darted out into traffic to photograph the Colosseum from the road. You never want to see one of your parents run over, especially not this early in the trip, but Dad managed to make it back to the sidewalk without being flattened by a Vespa.

saying coffee in Italy gets you only a steaming hot thimble of espresso. This was our sightseeing day, and after breakfast we ventured out into Eternal City. Our first stop was Trevi Fountain, which is located at the terminal point of the Acqua Vergine, one of the aqueducts that still provide Rome with pure water. In 1629 Pope Urban VIII decided the existing fountain was insufficiently dramatic, but after a contest and a redesign, it now stands more than eighty-six feet tall and is, by any standard, sufficiently dramatic. Water and depictions of Oceanus and Triton and Hippocamps flow seamlessly out from the Palazzo Poli, filling the square below, where hordes of tourists clamber to take photographs of themselves throwing coins into the fountain.[3]

I was jostling for position, my euro at the ready, when one of Rome's pigeons dropped a coin of his own right on my shoulder. And by coin, I mean poop. I looked away, gagging, while Mom rummaged through her purse searching for wipes and disinfectant. As she did, an older Italian man next to me laughed heartily and patted my shoulder saying, "Friend, this is a sign. A sign of good luck!"

"How do you figure?" I asked.

"Yes, today you are lucky," he said. "Soon you will get new clothes!"

Mom and Dad and the old man thought this was a lot funnier than I did.

Next we sat on the Spanish Steps, ranked number one on the UNESCO World Heritage list of greatest places to people watch. Then it was on to the Pantheon, home of the world's most famous leaky roof. And finally we strolled through the Piazza Navona, where we enjoyed margherita pizza and a life-changing dish of tiramisu at a little outdoor cafe, just before making a quick stop at San Luigi dei Francesi, to pay homage to Caravaggio's *The Calling of Saint Matthew*, my favorite painting that doesn't involve Bo Jackson.

That evening I had tickets for us to see SS Lazio (who along with AC Roma are the two top-flight soccer teams based in Rome) play AC

---

3. A coin tossed into the fountain is said to insure the visitor will one day return to Rome. An estimated three thousand euros are tossed into the fountain each day, earning more than $1.4 million a year that is used to subsidize a supermarket for Rome's needy.

Milan at the Stadio Olimpico in Rome. There were some rough-looking characters on our tram ride to the stadium, and I was a little concerned I was about to introduce my parents to soccer hooliganism, but the match was fantastic. There were five goals, three for the home side, and the fans sang and chanted for ninety minutes without taking a breath, my parents hardly flinching when a fan below us celebrated a Lazio goal by slamming himself headfirst into the glass wall that separated our section from the next. When there were just a few minutes left to play, we exited in the hope of catching a tram before they filled up, and, crossing the Tiber River, we could still hear chants from the stadium echoing into the cool Roman night.[4]

That night there was a lot of familiarity in the Stadio Olimpico for three people from an overwhelmingly Christian and football-obsessed part of the world. Soccer and Catholicism have become so intertwined in Italy that when Napoli won their first league championship in 1987, images of soccer star Diego Maradona were carried next to those of St. Januarius (the patron saint of Naples) during the procession of the Madonna dell'Arco. Of course, Italians would probably find it just as strange that in Alabama we sell decorative Christian crosses, orange and blue for Auburn fans, houndstooth or crimson for Alabama fans. Perhaps if America is heading in the direction of post-Christian Europe, the South will more closely resemble Italy, with Christian tradition blurring into the worship of sports.

On Sunday morning we took the metro back to the Spanish Steps, then walked a few hundred yards to the Piazza San Lorenzo, where the First Baptist Church of Rome sits next to a Louis Vuitton shop.

FBC Rome is a multicultural congregation with an English service on Sunday mornings at 10:30, followed throughout the day by a Filipino service, a Chinese service, and an Italian service. Inside, the church looks like any small Baptist church back home, with wooden pews and hymnals and a small pipe organ behind the pulpit. That morning we

---

4. Tricia wants me to mention that the tram running to our hotel had stopped running for the night, and my parents and I had to walk for miles through unfamiliar parts of Rome—but no one wants to read about that.

began with hymns and sang "It Is Well with My Soul" along with a congregation that appeared to be made up of people from around the world. And when guests were asked to introduce themselves, my assumption proved correct; I think every continent except for Antarctica was represented.

Protestants make up about 1.3 percent of the population in Italy, around 725,000, and from what I gathered, even that small number lives mostly in large cities. More than half of that 1.3 percent is made up of Assemblies of God, and if you took all the Baptists, Methodists, Lutherans, Presbyterians, and Anglicans in Italy and put them in the Rose Bowl, you'd think the game was a blowout because half the crowd had gone home.

Listening to the sermon at First Baptist Rome, I remembered that Dwight, a Facebook friend and an American Methodist living in Le Marche, told me, "It is impossible to be a practicing Protestant in Italy unless you live near a major city. The country, which polls at 95 percent Catholic, is quite unaware of what Protestantism means. I watch my home church in Kansas on streaming video and continue with a men's Bible study group back home via Skype on Fridays."

Others spoke to me about a fortress mentality that exists among evangelicals in Italy, and while this made me consider what my life would look like living in a predominantly Catholic country, it also made me consider, perhaps for the first time, what life must be like in Alabama for the few Catholics I know.

After church we ate pizza from a street vendor close to the Colosseum so Dad could retake all the pictures from two nights before in the daylight, then we took a tour of the Roman ruins and Palatine Hill, not to be confused with Palpatine Hill, which has something to do with Star Wars. Then it was time to see Vatican City.

I'm not sure how people will get from place to place in hell, but I imagine it will look a lot like the Rome metro. There are two lines, A and B, which crisscross the city. A third is rumored to be under construction, but apparently every time they start digging, they uncover an archeological treasure. So where most cities this size have a dozen or so metro lines, Rome has two, and they are crowded, and they are hot, and as with most hot and crowded places, they are kind of smelly.

That evening we took the metro to Vatican City, and as an overflowing train pulled up, I flashed back to a day two years earlier, and then I needed to sit down.

When Tricia and I visited, it was July, and it was hot, and most of my memories involve sweating. But one memory from that visit stands out above the rest; in fact it stands out above most of my memories. That's because it involves my right leg falling between a crowded metro train and the platform, my kneecap wedging tight between them, as people gasped and screamed and tried to pull me out before the train started up and ripped me in two. In the end, I didn't lose a leg, just a flip-flop, but the knot on my leg stayed with me for a couple of months, and the panicked feeling I get whenever I'm minding the gap will probably be with me forever. But you know what they say: "That which doesn't rip you in two makes for a good story."

That evening, we made it to the Vatican without one of us having to watch our intestines unwind as a metro train sped our torso away from our lower body. Standing in St. Peter's Square, I pointed the Sistine Chapel out to my parents, though we did not take the Vatican Museum tour, which allows you to tour the chapel and behold its famous painted ceiling. The reason I opted us out of this experience is because unless you get there early, which we weren't, the Vatican Museum is an overstuffed endless maze of priceless art and artifacts that you rush past trying to reach the Sistine Chapel. An hour later you are there, tired and out of breath, and you squeeze into the throng of other tired and out of breath tourists who, despite the signs asking them to remain silent and not take photographs, continue to talk loudly and take photographs. This causes the guards to shout "Silenzio!" every minute or so, making what could be an awe-filled and sacred experience one that cannot end soon enough.[5]

St. Peter's Square is actually a circle, a massive circle of marble

---

5. I just reread that paragraph. I don't expect the Vatican will ask me to write their travel brochures anytime soon.

columns with two openings, one filled with the enormity of St. Peter's Basilica, the other leading down the Via della Conciliazione, out of Vatican City and back into Rome. In the center stands a giant obelisk that Dan Brown probably has some thoughts on.

To enter St. Peter's Basilica, we waited in a long line that wrapped around the square. Security in Vatican City is high; you empty your pockets and walk through metal detectors like at an airport. There is also a dress code; women are not supposed to have bare shoulders, men should not wear short shorts, here or anywhere really. We figured this would make entry difficult for the man in front of us, who decided Daisy Dukes were appropriate for the occasion. But he actually slipped through the fashion police, in part because of a screaming baby who held everyone's attention. He did, however, receive some nasty looks from the men welcoming us to the basilica.

St. Peter's Basilica is an enormous space. It is longer than two football fields, wider than the distance from home plate to center field in any Major League Baseball park, and, at 452 feet, taller than the tallest building in seventeen states.[6]

We were in time for vespers at the Altar of the Chair, followed by Mass, and I watched as some of the faithful ducked under the velvet rope and made their way toward the chairs set up near the beautiful Chair of St. Peter in the basilica's apse. I stayed behind the rope, because I've always been a little intimidated by all things Catholic. And even though every Catholic I've ever spoken to has assured me I couldn't possibly mess up a service, my experience in the Russian Orthodox church had proved, at least to me, that I was entirely capable of doing just that. So I watched and listened to the lovely service from afar, closing my eyes as the beautiful hymns filled the giant basilica, and smiling to myself when I noticed the priest's voice echoing like Lou Gehrig's.

I don't think I will ever convert to Catholicism, because I'm not sure I could ever learn all the hand motions. But after spending time in Italy, I did want a better understanding of Catholicism, and of the

6. The tallest building in Vermont, Decker Towers, is only 124 feet tall. Come on, Vermont, dream bigger!

Catholic experience in the Bible Belt. I spoke to Father Victor Ingalls, associate pastor at St. Michael's Catholic Church back home in Auburn and an all-around nice guy. Fr. V, as he signs his emails, grew up in Montgomery and describes himself as the token Catholic kid. "I always heard about there being other Catholics in the world," he joked. Father Victor studied at the North American Pontifical College in Rome, and I asked him about his time there. "I had a whole new level of appreciation for my Catholicism when I was in Rome." Then he added, "I think any Christian who goes to Rome with the right lens walks away transformed. St. Peter's is this beautiful structure and all, but lying underneath it are the bones of a fisherman from the backwoods of Galilee."

I asked about Catholicism in Alabama, and Father Victor told me the Catholic Church is growing in the Deep South. "You can't casually be a Catholic here in the Deep South, because from about first grade on, you're getting bombarded with questions like, Why do you worship Mary? Why do you worship saints? Why are your parents drunk all the time? For me, because I was a minority, I was forced to ask myself those questions at an early age. What does it really mean to be a Catholic? And do I really want to live this out? Because it is not going to be convenient. And now, you walk around Auburn with a collar and you get a lot of funny looks. A few weeks ago the girl at Chipotle couldn't stop laughing, and when I asked what was so funny, she said, "I just can't believe I'm making a burrito for a priest." I told her to believe it, because it was happening.

I liked Father Victor a lot, even after I found out we cheer for rival college football teams, and I found it interesting that he used the word convenient. It was certainly convenient for me to grow up a Baptist, yet I thought of the Catholics as the ones just going through the motions (pun intended). Generally speaking, people don't just go through the motions unless it's convenient. Persecution, or even mild ridicule, is generally enough to make someone drop a belief they don't truly believe. Say what you will about Catholics in the South, but they're not Catholic because it's easy.

That said, I've heard many Protestants say that Catholicism in

Italy is more about heritage than anything else, but since I've heard Protestants say that about all Catholics everywhere most of my life, I took it with a grain of salt. However, Father Victor agreed, saying, "For many it's become just part of being Italian."

Patrizia, an Italian woman Father Victor introduced me to, confirmed this—sort of—when I spoke to her over the phone. "There are things I don't approve of in the Catholic Church," she said, "but I would never change my religion, because changing my religion, to me, would be like changing my nationality." But then she turned the stereotype on its head when she spoke about her time living in Alabama. "In Italy I was able to go to church more often because there are more Catholic churches, and consequently more Masses. I was able to go to church every day in Italy, and I miss that living here."

Because of travel, I have learned not to paint with such a broad brush, because inevitably I have met people like Patrizia who don't match my preconceived notions. That said, we're talking about a country where, if poll numbers are to be believed, there are fifty-three million professing Catholics, yet only forty-three million people who say they believe in God. So obviously, for some, saying they are Catholic is just another way of saying they are Italian. But are Christians in the South any different?

Take my home state of Alabama. In religious surveys, we always rank among the most Christian states. However, our divorce rate ranks just as high, and our online pornography viewing statistics are no better, and sometimes actually higher than those of the "heathens" in the "godless states" to our north and west.

■ ■ ■

The next morning, we left Rome by train, heading north to Pisa, where Dad took the obligatory photograph of Mom holding up the leaning tower with her pinky, then we traveled up the western coast of Italy toward Genoa. The views were simply stunning, as the Ligurian Sea crashed into the rocky coastline, just below the multicolored villages overlooking it all. I wanted to stop and spend a week in every town we passed.

We changed trains in Genoa, and it was there, standing on a train platform, that my phone buzzed with a text message from Tricia. She'd just had her first ultrasound, and there on my phone was a photograph of our son, who slightly resembled a seahorse. I stared at that picture for the rest of the trip and wondered whether I could ever feel farther away from home.

We had only one full day in Milan, so we woke early and walked to the city center, passing through the lovely Parco Sempione as we went. Eventually we found ourselves in front of the Milan Cathedral, which dominates the main city square. It was a lovely morning, and we sat on the front steps of the cathedral, people watching.

Next to Milan Cathedral is the Galleria Vittorio Emanuele II, the world's oldest shopping mall. Two intersecting glass-vaulted arcades make up the mall that houses Gucci, Prada, and many other expensive stores Tricia did not get a souvenir from. The mosaic floors of the Galleria are of particular interest, especially the bull depicting the Turin coat of arms. Legend has it that if you place your right heel on the bull's testicles and spin around three times, you will have good luck. Though when I did this, my sunglasses went soaring through the air, landing with many new scratches on the beautiful floor.

After inhaling a plate of spaghetti alla carbonara so delicious I regretted ever eating at Olive Garden, we met up with our tour group in front of the cathedral. Generally I despise tour groups, but a tour group is just about the only way to see Leonardo da Vinci's *The Last Supper*, which has a very limited viewing each day. So to see the famed painting, we had to see the rest of Milan with twenty-five strangers and a very, very energetic woman wearing a microphone headset and carrying a stuffed animal on a stick so we wouldn't lose sight of her.

We revisited the Milan Cathedral, then the Galleria, each of the group taking turns spinning on the bull's balls, then we spent some time in Milan Castle before arriving at the Convent of Santa Maria delle Grazie, where one of the cafeteria walls is adorned with the most famous painting in the world.

Around twenty-five people are allowed to see the painting every fifteen minutes, which makes it more difficult to see than the Sistine Chapel, but also makes for an infinitely nicer viewing experience. We all sat in a waiting room, then were ushered down a hall and passed through some vacuum-sealed holding cells before finally a door buzzed and we poured out into the large empty room, where we were confronted by the masterpiece.

The first thing people usually tell you after they've seen *The Mona Lisa* is, "It's much smaller than I imagined." That is not the case with *The Last Supper.* Fifteen feet tall, and nearly twenty-nine feet across, the mural dominates the room and demands your attention.

Can sitting and gawking at a painting be a holy experience? I don't know, but I know Da Vinci's masterpiece was for my eyes what hearing Handel's *Messiah* is for my ears. And standing there in front of that five-hundred-year-old painting, it was impressed on me that Christians have been worshiping Christ for a long, long time. And were I able to trace my Christian heritage all the way back to Christ, it undoubtedly would pass through many faithful Catholics.

As Father Victor said to me later, "You're writing this book, and you're exploring the different expressions of Christianity around the world. But that reality you're exploring exists because these twelve guys followed this itinerant preacher in the Middle East. And somehow this fisherman Peter worked his way to Rome, the center of the Western world, and is martyred, and this whole enterprise is still going two thousand years later."

Fifteen minutes later, our time with *The Last Supper* was up, and I took my parents on one last exhausting trek through Milan back to our hotel. The next morning, we were on a plane back home, back to the Bible Belt, back to my pregnant wife, and back to the comfort of being a Protestant in a land of Protestants. But after you travel, things are never the same. Within minutes of landing, my mom's cell phone rang, and much to my surprise and delight, she answered with a hearty "buongiorno!"

JAPAN

Domo arigato, Mr. Roboto.
—Styx, "Mr. Roboto"

"Welcome aboard, Mr. Gibbs. May I offer you a predeparture glass of champagne?"

"Sure," I said. "Why not?" Then I glanced over at Brian Brown, my college friend who now works in Auburn's college of agriculture and was accepting a predeparture beverage of his own, and I smiled.

I wasn't looking forward to the cramped fourteen-hour flight from Atlanta to Tokyo, but during the booking process, I realized I had enough frequent flier miles to fly first class. However, it seemed wrong for me to fly first class while Brian was stuck back in coach, so instead I booked two one-way first class tickets to Tokyo, and then I was dreading only the cramped fourteen-hour flight home. And I suppose I could spend a great deal of this chapter telling you about the wine tour at thirty-seven thousand feet, or the caviar, or the filet mignon for dinner, or the hot fudge sundaes for dessert, or Bose headphones, or the amenity kits, or the free pajamas, or getting to fly the plane, or the lie-flat seats with mattresses, blankets, and pillows, or any number of things that made that flight the nicest travel experience I'd ever had, but I should probably leave it at one paragraph and move on.

Seriously, though, international first class is awesome.[1]

■ ■ ■

We landed at Narita International Airport around 4:00 p.m. local time the next day, and we boarded the Narita Express, the train that took us to Shinjuku Station in Tokyo, the busiest rail station in the solar system.

The airport in Narita is sometimes called Tokyo Narita International Airport, which is a little like calling Atlanta's airport the Tokyo Atlanta International Airport. It took more than an hour to reach Tokyo, and we were on an express train. Dragging our luggage behind us, we disembarked into a sea of Japanese humanity. Never in my life have I seen so many people in one place. Currents and undertows of bodies pulled and pushed us across the station, finally throwing us against a wall, where we stood, mouths agape, just watching the madness flow past

1. Seriously awesome.

us. Brian looked at me and said, "It looks just like when you step in an ant bed."

More than 3.64 million people pass through Shinjuku Station every day, and it felt like the majority of today's 3.64 million decided to all come at once. To put this in perspective, let's just assume these commuters come in ten-minute increments. That means every ten minutes, 25,277 people pass through the station. It's a busy train station.

By the grace of God, we found our way out of Shinjuku Station and were confronted by lights brighter than those in Times Square. Brian and I stopped for photographs, not realizing every other intersection in Tokyo looks like this. From there it was a short walk to our hotel, and we passed many people wearing surgical masks, which at first is a little disconcerting, considering we were in the part of the world where weird viruses often seem to originate. Later we found out it is a common courtesy in Japan to wear a surgical mask when *you* have a cold, so you won't spread your germs to others, which is actually quite considerate.

Brian and I checked into our hotel room, not really knowing what day our bodies thought it was, but thankful that we were sleepy and it was nighttime and somehow we had defeated the evil forces of jet lag just this once. But before crashing, we watched a few minutes of Japanese television, which is mesmerizing. The live shows always seemed to have flashing or scrolling text on at least three sides of the screen, with the fourth side reserved for a small circle where a person's disembodied head reacts to whatever is happening in the middle, which currently was an overweight man consuming a chocolate covered snowman with a large wooden spoon. Watching these shows, combined with their commercials, which are akin to the strangest dreams you've ever had on cough medicine, I wondered if Japanese television's primary function isn't to bewilder foreigners.

Before the trip, I exchanged emails with Con Wilson, a friend from college who spent time as a missionary in Japan, and lying in bed looking out at the Tokyo skyline, I recalled some of our conversation. I'd asked Con about misconceptions Americans might have about Japan, and he laughed and said, "That they are all good at math. That they all know kung fu, which is Chinese martial arts, by the way." Con's wife, Chiyo, is Japanese, and looking back, I get the feeling Con is so close to Japanese culture he probably wasn't the best person to prepare me for the culture shock I felt there. By now he probably thinks Japanese television is perfectly normal. But Con was able to shed some light on what it's like living in Japan as an American missionary.

"As a Caucasian missionary, it is actually fairly easy in Japan," Con said. "Caucasians have an easier time sharing the gospel in Japan, easier than a Japanese national sharing the gospel with another Japanese. Japanese will listen to internationals share their faith because it's an opportunity to practice English and a chance to better understand American culture, as they believe all Americans are Christians. That said, I think it takes a rare type of missionary to really thrive in Japan. I've had a few friends who just cannot adjust to the cultural differences."

I'd never really thought about a missionary's ability to thrive in a foreign culture, though I suppose if you never adjust to everyday life, it would be difficult to plug in to a community and share Christ. Before turning out the lights, I looked over my guidebook's list of cultural differences between Japan and the US, and I wasn't sure how well I'd thrive in Japan either. Particularly after reading that witty banter and sarcasm with strangers can be considered a personal attack. Witty banter and sarcasm with strangers is my go-to form of communication, which leads me to believe I'd probably last about a week in Japan.

The next morning, we spent some time acclimating ourselves to the Tokyo subway, which is made up of two separate systems, the Tokyo metro, and the Tokyo Metropolitan Bureau of Transportation (Toei). This was confusing, but not nearly as confusing as the metro map, which I believe was drawn by the president of the Bureau of Transportation's two-year-old daughter. Of course, only Brian and I appeared to be struggling with this, so maybe it wasn't the two-year-old's fault.

Our first stop was the Ryogoku Sumo Hall, a thirteen-thousand-seat sporting arena that was hosting the Hatsu Basho, the first of six official professional sumo tournaments in Japan each year. We paid twenty dollars for general admission seats and walked inside to an almost empty arena.

"I'm bigger than those guys," Brian said, pointing down at the ring where two scantily clad little wrestlers were pushing each other around the dohyo.

"Tricia is bigger than those guys," I said.

Turned out these tournaments last fifteen days, and apparently the huge wrestlers people want to watch don't fight until later in the evening. I don't think sumo wrestling will threaten the NFL in the US anytime soon, but we enjoyed the two hours we spent watching, in part because of the spectacle of it all (particularly the referee's singing introduction of each wrestler), but mostly because the concession stand sold delicious yakitori, which is basically grilled chicken on a stick.

After we'd had our fill of sumo wrestling (and yakitori), we made our way over to the Tokyo Skytree, a broadcasting and observation tower which, at 2080 feet, is the second tallest structure in the world, behind Burj Khalifa in Dubai. Skytree had been open less than a year when we visited, and the line to visit the first observation deck was close to an hour,[2] so we waited our turn among what looked like mostly Japanese tourists. Eventually we were crammed into a space-age elevator that zipped us up to the first deck, and stepping out into the glass room, we were grateful we waited in line. The city appeared to go on for miles in every direction. We knew it was big; with more than thirty-five million residents, it's the largest metro area in the world,[3] but it wasn't until we saw it from this vantage point that either of us grasped just how big. Throw in the sun setting behind Mt. Fuji in the distance and you've got one of the most amazing sights on the planet.

"I could stay up here forever," I said.

"It is beautiful," Brian said, then added, "Can you imagine being up here during an earthquake?"

"Never mind, I'm ready to go."

---

2. The first deck is 350 meters up. A second one is 450 meters, but you have to pay extra.

3. The Tokyo Metropolitan Area would be the second largest state in the United States, behind California, and has more people than Wyoming, Vermont, North Dakota, Alaska, South Dakota, Delaware, Montana, Rhode Island, New Hampshire, Maine, Hawaii, Idaho, West Virginia, Nebraska, New Mexico, Nevada, Utah, Kansas, Arkansas, Mississippi, Iowa, and Connecticut combined.

That evening we ventured out to Akihabara, aka Electric Town, where on Sunday evenings the main thoroughfare is blocked off and the street fills with Japanese anime cosplayers.

And now a couple of definitions for the uninitiated.

a·nime /ˈanəˌmā/ (noun): Japanese movie and television animation, often having a science fiction theme and sometimes including violent or explicitly sexual material.

cosplay /ˈkɒzpleɪ/ (noun): the practice of dressing up as a character from a film, book, or video game, especially one from the Japanese genres of manga or anime.

Unfortunately for us, this was Friday night, not Sunday, but there was still plenty to see in Electric Town, including more than a few people in costume. The buildings were covered in vividly colored, brightly lit advertisements for video games or anime movies or some new electronic device. The temperature was hovering around thirty, yet there were people everywhere, including young girls wearing very little clothing, handing out advertisement flyers to the young men walking by. These young men, from what I gathered, have a particular fetish for cartoon depictions of teenage girls with enormous breasts, a look the advertising girls were trying to replicate with varying degrees of success. Brian and I ducked into a store that contained nothing but those claw games where you deposit a dollar and try to grab a prize, the prizes here being anime DVDs or statues of teenage cartoon girls with enormous breasts. This particular claw game store was four stories tall and jam-packed with people losing their yen. From there we browsed a couple of electronics stores that sold every device and accessory you could imagine. One store had an entire floor devoted to iPhone cases. Electric Town was one of those places that was so wonderfully weird I could have stayed for hours, but we had to be up early the next morning, so we called it a night.

Saturday morning we skipped the twenty-five dollar hotel breakfast, opting instead for the Burger King next door and the promise of sausage biscuits. I always feel a twinge of guilt eating American fast food in foreign countries, but I do think you learn something about a culture by eating their version of Burger King or McDonald's. For instance, I learned that in Japan a sausage biscuit consists of a hamburger patty, the most bizarre-looking fried egg I've ever seen, a hamburger bun, and all of the mayonnaise they can find. One bite later, I was buying a pack of powdered donuts from the convenience store next door.

After breakfast Brian and I made our way to Tokyo Station, home of the Shinkansen bullet trains. Before boarding we walked to the end of the train to look at what I guess you'd call the engine, and oh, my word, it looked more like a rocket you'd use to explore distant planets than a commuter train. We took our seats and the train began creeping through the urban sprawl of Tokyo, accelerating a little into the suburban sprawl, and without even realizing it had happened, we were hurtling through the Japanese countryside at 185 mph. Our ride lasted about two and a half hours, and soon we were hopping off in Nagoya, a city I'd never heard of before this trip and which, despite my ignorance, has a metro area population of 8.9 million people, more than forty of our fifty states.

Nagoya Station, like everywhere else we went in Japan, was really crowded, and we just stood in the middle of it all, waiting to be found by Pastor Shinichiro Saito. During my college days at Auburn, I met Shinichiro while he was a seminary intern at Lakeview Baptist. I still remember how he taught me to pronounce his name, pointing to his shin, then scratching like he was itching all over, then pretending to row a boat. Shinichiro and his wife, Shoko, moved back to Japan in 2000, and for two years he was the pastor of Shinkoiwa Baptist Church in Tokyo. In 2002 they moved to Nagoya, and Shinichiro has served as pastor of Hirabari Baptist Church ever since.

Now, I'm not trying to imply here that all Japanese people look the same (they do not), but I did not like our odds of picking out a man I hadn't seen in more than a decade among the masses in Nagoya Station. Thankfully, picking us out in a crowded Japanese train station was not difficult at all, and soon a man was tapping my shoulder and asking, "Are you looking for Pastor Saito?" It was Shinichiro, and we tossed our bags into his van and soon we were driving through the busy city center.

"We will eat dinner soon, but first I have a history lesson for you," Shinichiro said, and he drove us to Nagoya Castle, a breathtaking four-hundred-year-old Japanese castle in the center of the city.

Shinichiro paid our admission, and as we entered the first level, he said, "I will tell why Christianity struggles in Japan." As we walked around the first floor full of murals and models, Shinichiro explained that a large majority of Japanese do not identify with a particular religion. Most polls put this number between 70 and 80 percent. However, almost the same high percentage of Japanese are considered Buddhist or Shinto or a combination of the two, but this number comes from birth records or other loose associations, not a confession of faith. "Buddhists and Shintos believe that converting to Christianity angers your ancestors, who in turn might curse your entire family. So not just immediate families but all relatives often oppose a family member becoming a Christian. Also, only Buddhists are typically allowed to visit a Buddhist gravesite, so if one becomes a Christian, they will likely not be allowed to visit their family grave or be buried with their family."

The second floor was full of Samurai swords and extraordinarily long rifles with curved stocks. I asked Shinichiro if this was the Tom Cruise era of Japanese history, but I don't think he'd seen *The Last Samurai*. He did say that "for decades Japanese have been told that European countries tried to use Christianity to rule over Japan, to make Japan like the other Western colonies in Asia. We learn about Western history and Christian countries constantly fighting each other. Many Japanese do not trust religion because of all the killing that was done in the name of religion in the past."

As I've mentioned earlier, I often wonder how much involvement Christians should have in the political arena. I've read opinions across the spectrum and find compelling arguments on every side, but I do think Christians should be concerned with what their government does in the name of Christ. Perhaps this isn't as much an issue now as it was during the European colonial period, when church and state worked hand in hand to convert souls and increase trade, though usually not in that order. But in America we are quick to associate our perfect God with our very imperfect country. And though most Christians would probably say we are far from a Christian nation, the rest of the world often views us as such. Spain and Portugal's actions from hundreds of years ago are still hindering the gospel in Japan today. I don't think it hurts to ask whether our country is doing things today that will thwart the expansion of the gospel in years to come.

We finally made it to the top floor of the castle, and I was mentally and physically exhausted from all the climbing and history, but the view was amazing, and while we caught our breath, Shinichiro told us that Sunday in Japan is for clubs and sports and weddings and traveling, and how it is almost against Japanese culture to attend church each Sunday. He then told us about the outrageous price of real estate in Japan, and how most churches are small and out of the way and hard to find.

Con mentioned some of this before my trip, saying, "The average Japanese will go to a temple a couple of times a year and practice rituals at funerals, and maybe some holidays. This style of religion fits nicely into their busy work schedules. Christianity requires so much more time and commitment, and I believe that is a big factor in the lack of interest from the majority of the populace."

As we looked out on the city of Nagoya from atop the castle, Shinichiro told us even the concept of hell works against Christianity in Japan. "Many Japanese think of hell as a place most go after they die. It is not bad news for Japanese to go to hell, but rather natural. They have trouble distinguishing between heaven and hell, so a Japanese person might react, 'What's the big deal of going to hell? My ancestors are there too.'"

I remembered Con saying, "There's a famous saying in Japan, 'The nail that sticks out gets hammered down.' So for a Japanese to step out and become a Christian marks them as different. Even if no other Japanese pressure them, they still feel a sense of pressure within themselves. On top of this, Christianity already looks incredibly fragmented from a Japanese perspective, and if we are honest, it *is* fragmented. So when a Japanese converts to Christianity, they look to move into a Christian community, but upon closer inspection, they see all these different types of churches and people telling them which ones they should or should not attend. For the Japanese, it is particularly disconcerting."

I told Shinichiro that it has always been easy for me to look at a place like Japan and just assume Christianity struggles because most people belong to another religion. And sure, Buddhist tradition and beliefs are a roadblock to the gospel in Japan, but the issue is more complex than that, and it was fascinating to hear some of the reasons Christians make up only 1–2 percent of the Japanese population, even though the country is open for missionaries and not particularly hostile toward believers.

"This is a difficult place for Christianity to thrive," Shinichiro said as we began to make our way back downstairs, "but God does special things in difficult places."

Snow was falling when we walked out of the castle, and the three of us stood in a courtyard taking in the beautiful scene. But like most snowy days, the beauty of it all was eclipsed by the coldness of it all, so we headed for the van. On our way, we passed a street vendor selling dorayaki, and Shinichiro insisted we have some, telling us it was pancakes filled with red beans and sugar. I know this sounds like a recipe made from Mad Libs, but it was actually quite delicious.

That evening Shinichiro took us to what I suppose is the Japanese version of Olive Garden, not because the food was Italian but because you could have all the soup and salad you wanted. I ordered a chicken dish, and Shinichiro, Brian, and the waitress all took turns helping me use chopsticks, but it never took. They kept saying, "Hold this one the way you hold a pencil," which doesn't help at all because I hold a pencil in a very peculiar way, and when I try to hold a pencil, or chopsticks, like the rest of the population, my hand begins to cramp in a matter of minutes. The waitress brought me a fork.

The snow was falling hard by the time we reached Shinichiro's church, Hirabari Baptist Church, located in a quiet (by Japanese standards) part of town, around eight miles east of Nagoya Station. We'd been told we could sleep in the church that evening, and when we walked inside, we were struck by an arctic blast that made me wonder how the inside of the church could actually be colder than the snowy night outside. The church was made even colder when we were asked to remove our shoes at the door and slip on a pair of red slippers that had been waiting for us. I feared providing guests with subzero sleeping conditions was some sort of Japanese custom I'd not been familiar with, but thankfully there were heaters on upstairs where our beds had been made in the nursery. That night we prayed with Shinichiro for his church and for the future of Christianity in Japan, then we slept like babies in the nursery.

The next morning, Shinichiro, Shoko, and their two children met us in the church kitchen, where Shoko prepared a wonderful breakfast of bacon, eggs, clam chowder, and some of the best strawberries I've ever tasted. Later that week at a market, we noticed twelve strawberries on sale for thirty dollars, leaving us feeling slightly guilty for not acting more appreciative of the apparent delicacy we'd received.

After breakfast Shinichiro took us on a chilly prayer walk through his neighborhood. The snow had almost melted and the city was just waking up as Shinichiro pointed out schools and other landmarks. On our walk, I began to gain a little understanding of what it must be like for Christians in Japan. Until now I'd only been to countries where Christians make up a majority of the population, even if the majority of the population doesn't consider themselves practicing Christians. If you tell someone in England you are a Christian, most likely they will have some idea of what that means. This does not seem to be the case in Japan, and these small churches, and most of them are quite small, operate as little islands in a vast sea of unbelief. Obviously I cannot speak for every church in Japan, but Hirabari Baptist does not seem hampered by its smallness. Instead, the church has adopted a laserlike focus on impacting the surrounding community for Christ. As we walked, Shinichiro pointed out houses where church members live, houses where children who occasionally visit the church live, and houses where families that had been invited to church live. At Nagoya Castle, when Shinichiro detailed the difficulties Christianity faces in

Japan, I felt depressed. The odds against Christianity ever thriving here seemed so long, and I wondered where you would ever start. But Jesus told us to love God and love our neighbors, and that is exactly what Shinichiro is doing. He told us he walks these streets often, praying for the families inside each home, and I thought it was beautiful to see a pastor so focused on the families within earshot of his church's bells.

Our walk lasted close to an hour, and we made it back just in time for children's church. Walking upstairs at the church, we could hear the children singing, and we stood in the back until they finished. There were about five of them, including Shinichiro's son and daughter, and we were asked to sit in front of them and field questions. At first the questions were easy, and somewhat repetitive. Shinichiro translated.

"He asks, 'When is your birthday?'"

"She asks, 'When is your wife's birthday?'"

"He asks, 'When is your anniversary?'"

"June 18," I said, and the kids screamed with glee. I looked at Shinichiro, confused, and he said, "One of their birthdays is also June 18."

But then the questions got a little tougher.

"He asks, 'How many Bible verses have you memorized?'"

"She asks, 'How many people have you led to Christ?'"

I was waiting for Shinichiro to say, "They ask, 'How are babies made?'"

After snacks we walked downstairs to the sanctuary, where people were gathering for the Sunday service. In all there were about twenty-five people in attendance, and Brian and I sat on the back row, wondering if Baptists in Japan would do the same. The service began and we sang "How Great Thou Art," my grandfather James' favorite hymn, Brian and I singing in English, the rest of the congregation in Japanese.

I couldn't help but think about my grandfather and all the other men and women from the World War II generation. Would they ever have dreamed their grandchildren would be attending a Baptist church in Japan, singing hymns alongside Japanese believers?

Shinichiro's sermon was excellent, no doubt, though I cannot say for sure because it was in Japanese, which I do not speak, and the notes did not help much either, because they too were in Japanese, which I do not read. However, I did gather from the slide presentation that the sermon had something to do with Rick Warren's *The Purpose Driven Life*.

After the service, everyone went upstairs for what I guess you'd call Sunday school, though it was really just all of us sitting around a table and Shinichiro translating questions from the members. This group skipped asking our birthdays, instead asking about our lives back home, where we go to church, when we became Christians, and what are some of the issues facing the church in America.

Brian mentioned abortion, and Shinichiro translated his thoughts around the table. Then someone asked us if the church is involved in the gun control debate.

Japan has extremely strict gun control measures in place—the biathletes in the 1998 Nagano Olympics had to go through retina scans before picking up their rifles—and I got the feeling most of the people in the room think the church should be on the side of stricter gun control. I also knew Brian has the exact opposite view, so I kicked up my feet to enjoy the debate.

Brian began by saying the right to bear arms is guaranteed by our constitution and that he owns three guns for hunting and protection. Shinichiro translated this and eyes widened around the room.

I asked the congregation if they thought of America as a dangerous place, and heads began to bob up and down. "No," Brian said, "it's just that you guys see only the worst parts of America on the news. Just because there are guns doesn't mean America is a dangerous place to live."

Then a little woman in the back raised her hand, asked something in Japanese, and then the translation came from Shinichiro. "She asks, 'If America is not dangerous, why do you need three guns for protection?'"

I laughed out loud and Brian just smiled, chalking up the argument to a loss in translation.

After question and answer time, a lunch of bowl after bowl of

Japanese deliciousness was served. There was smoked salmon sushi, fried tofu dumplings with noodles, a bowl of orange swirly stuff, something that looked like cabbage, and a bowl of soup that looked too simple to taste as amazing as it did. The ladies of the church tried their best to teach me to master chopsticks, but eventually gave up. However, I totally mastered the Japanese method of eating soup, which is just to slurp it straight from the bowl. Tricia does not like that this is now the only way I will eat cereal.

On the train ride home that evening, we enjoyed absolutely stunning views of Mt. Fuji. Brian and I ran up and down the train, trying to find open windows to take photographs from, while the rest of our train mates slept or played with their phones. It's amazing what people just get used to seeing.

That night I slept hard until around 4:30 a.m., when Brian screamed, "Chad! Do you feel that?" I woke up, sat up, and realized the earth was moving more than it typically does. "I think it's an earthquake," Brian said. And it was. A 5.1 earthquake centered a little north of Tokyo. We both pulled up Twitter and searched for tweets from Tokyo and found hundreds from Japanese people angry that another earthquake had kept them from a good night's sleep. I was feeling a lot of emotions at the time, but anger was not one of them. Sure, I live in a part of the world where about once a month the sky turns green, starts spinning, and sucks entire towns into oblivion, but at least the earth doesn't shake! Needless to say, neither of us slept well the rest of the night. The earthquake had not felt like I'd always imagined an earthquake would feel. It was a strange, unnatural feeling, and I'm not in a hurry to ever feel it again.

The next morning, we were shaken, literally and figuratively, but we did manage to leave the hotel, and after lunch we visited Senso-ji, an ancient Buddhist temple in Toyko that was founded in 628.[4] To get to the temple, we walked down the Nakamise-Dori, a narrow street lined with close to one hundred shops and vendors. The Nakamise-Dori

---

4. The current building isn't that ancient. In fact it's about the same age as our house in Auburn, because its predecessor was bombed and destroyed during World War II.

is packed shoulder to shoulder with people before opening up at the magnificent Thunder Gate, which you pass through to enter the temple grounds.

Inside, there were tourists and pilgrims and school tours, many stopping at a large incense burner, wafting the smoke into their faces. We watched as dozens of young schoolgirls stopped at the incense burner, and I was reminded of a friend who asked whether my travels were shifting my beliefs more toward universalism.

I thought it was a fair question, because when you go out and see the world, it's a question you'll likely ask yourself. Because you are going to meet faithful Buddhists and Hindus and Muslims, and when they talk about their beliefs, they are going to sound a lot like you do when you talk about your beliefs. You'll wonder how they feel inside when they pray. You'll wonder how comforted they are by their beliefs during difficult times. And you'll probably start to think, Who am I to say these people won't be in heaven? And you know, if I get to heaven and there are Buddhists and Hindus and Muslims, I think that will be about the greatest thing ever. But like I told my friend, I still want these people to know about Jesus.

That evening, we stood for an hour outside a packed one-room restaurant called Harajuku Gyoza Lou, waiting for what we'd read were the best dumplings in town. Of course, I haven't tried all the other dumplings in Tokyo, but the steamed pork dumplings we had that night were cheap and delicious and certainly better than the lunch we'd had at Denny's. Then after dinner we went to an intersection just to watch people cross the street. Of course, it wasn't just any intersection; Shibuya Crossing was featured in the Bill Murray film *Lost in Translation* and is just about the craziest thing I've ever seen. A busy five-way intersection screeches to a halt, and for forty-five seconds, hundreds of pedestrians make a mad dash across the road. It looks like a flash mob every time the light turns red, and Brian and I joined in the fun three or four times before securing window seats on the second floor of the Shibuya Starbucks so we could watch the madness for another hour.

The next day was our last in Japan, and we spent the morning milling around Tokyo Station, where a woman handed me a sample of what looked like caramel on a toothpick, but turned out to be octopus innards, which taste nothing, and I mean nothing, like caramel. Then it was back on the Narita Express to the airport. We watched the sun set on the Land of the Rising Sun before boarding our long, fourteen-hour flight to Chicago. A flight made even longer by the fact that we were in coach, our first class carriage turning into a pumpkin when my frequent flier miles ran out. Touching down in Chicago after half a day in a plane, we sat and watched the sun set for the second time that Tuesday, both of us getting dizzier the more we thought about it. So we zonked out in front of a television while waiting on our connection home and watched a show about bearded men who make duck calls. It was good to be back in a place where television isn't weird.

THE NETHERLANDS

Baby went to Amsterdam
Four, five days for the Big Canal

—Peter Bjorn and John,
"Amsterdam"

While packing for my trip to the Netherlands, it struck me that only four years ago, I'd never even left the southeastern United States, and here I was preparing for my eighth trip to Europe. I felt like a seasoned traveler at this point, with my clothes rolled perfectly for maximum capacity, my credit card companies notified of my travel plans, and my travel documents printed and stowed for easy accessibility. So it was a bit of a shock, and just a touch humbling, when five miles from the Atlanta airport, I stopped for gas only to realize my wallet was still sitting on my nightstand, just where I'd left it. Good grief.

This mishap cost me three hours, $150 to change the flight, and a huge favor from my friend Scott Stevenson, who met me at the state line with my wallet, but I eventually made it to Philadelphia, where I joined three dudes I'd met on the internet. Sorry, that sounded kind of sketchy. I joined Tyler Stanton, a famous YouTube personality and one half of the Tripp and Tyler comedy duo; Bryan Allain, a writer and podcaster and comedian who loves the Red Sox more than you love your wife; and Joseph Craven, a guy with a beard from Mississippi. And while technically I did meet all of these guys on the internet, I now consider them real friends, as opposed to e-friends, I guess.

Our flight was to Brussels, Belgium, and upon landing, we ate Belgian waffles covered in chocolate syrup before boarding a train to Antwerp, then another train to Amsterdam. The only excitement came when Bryan lost his train ticket, the rest of us secretly wanting to see the conductor throw him off the moving train. They never even asked for his ticket, though, so we settled into our comfy seats, and the rest of the ride through the Netherlands passed in a sleepy blur. Every once in a while someone would say, "Hey, a windmill," and I'd wake up to see an old wooden windmill and flat land as far as the eye could see. I don't really even remember arriving at Amsterdam's Centraal Station or the tram ride to our hotel, but I do recall voting for naps over sightseeing. Three hours later, we met back in the lobby and had dinner at the little pub next door overlooking a sleepy canal.

The next morning, we met downstairs in the lobby and watched through the window as dozens of bundled up Nederlanders passed on bicycles. I can't imagine a more cycling friendly country than the

Netherlands. You are confronted with it as soon as you walk out of Amsterdam Centraal and see, by my estimation, seven trillion bicycles parked on the canal front. Nearly 60 percent of all trips in Dutch cities are made on bicycles, and as we stood in the lobby, delaying the freezing search for breakfast we were about to embark on, men and women from just about every age group pedaled past.[1] Not having wheels of our own, we hit the pavement at a brisk pace, looking for anything edible.

The four of us ducked inside the first coffee house we saw, and by coffee house I mean a cafe that serves only coffee and pastries. I have to clarify here because in the Netherlands, shops that legally sell marijuana for personal consumption along with coffee are called coffee shops, while shops that sell coffee but do not offer marijuana are called coffee houses, which I can only assume has led to some confusion for the caffeine seeking foreigner. We sat inside by a warm fire and drank our weight in coffee, our resolve to go outside and do something weakening with each rosy-cheeked person that came shivering through the door. But eventually we roused our courage and took a tram to Dam Square, in the heart of Amsterdam.

At Dam Square, we stood between the Royal Palace and National Monument, dodging trams and pigeons, before eventually picking a direction at random and walking just to stay warm. But soon the sun rose above the buildings and shined down warmly on our backs, slowing our pace and brightening our moods.

Amsterdam is a major air hub in Europe, and I'd had three daylong stopovers there before this, my fourth, visit. I don't think I could ever get tired of walking through the city's famous canal ring area. There are more than one hundred kilometers of canals in Amsterdam, the major canals forming large concentric half circles. Sometimes called the Venice of the North, Amsterdam feels much more organized than its Italian counterpart. In Venice you wander alongside canals, feeling more lost with every step. In Amsterdam I always feel like I'm going in the right direction, even when I don't know where I'm going.

---

1. During World War II, Germans confiscated all the bicycles in Holland, and to this day, whenever the Netherlands play Germany in soccer, Dutch fans chant, "Give us back our bicycles!"

For lunch we stopped at a place called Winkel 43, because we'd been told they have the best apple pie in this or any galaxy. Located near the Noordermarkt, in the Amsterdam Jewish quarter called Jordaan, Winkel 43 had customers flowing out its doors when we arrived. So we waited, eventually securing seats at the bar and ordering club sandwiches. Then came the apple pie, topped high with whipped cream. Now, I hate watching television shows about food because no matter how many times you lick your TV, you cannot taste what's on the screen. And I understand writing about food is really no better, so before you lick this page, I want to warn you it will taste like thin sheets of pulpwood. But let me just say this: twelve months later I still occasionally check flight prices to Amsterdam just so I can have another slice of pie from Winkel.[2]

After lunch we walked toward the towering spire of Westerkerk (Western Church), passing over the Prinsengracht canal on one of Amsterdam's fifteen hundred bridges. We had reserved tickets to visit the Anne Frank House, which sits in the shadow of Westerkerk, and were thankful we did, since the line, even on this frigid day, was wrapped around the building. With thirty minutes to kill before our tour, we stepped inside the warmth of the old church, craning our necks to look up at the nearly four-hundred-year-old pipe organ that was being played, I suppose, strictly for our entertainment. "Just think," Bryan said, "generations of Christians have sat in these pews, marveling at this majestic organ, instagramming the whole thing." We instagrammed it ourselves before signing our friend Knox's name in the guest book and walking next door for our tour.

Here I'm going to assume you've read Anne Frank's *The Diary of a Young Girl*. If you haven't, you're going to need to put this book down and go read it now. Tricia and I had visited the Anne Frank House a few months earlier on our way home from Uganda,[3] and I'm not sure I've been in a more powerful and moving museum. Anne's diary came to life as I stepped through hidden doors and climbed up narrow passages,

---

2. Bryan passed on the apple pie, later admitting it was the worst €3 he ever saved.

3. That night, Tricia and I stayed at the Amsterdam Hilton. If you are a Beatles fan, you know how awesome that is.

passing through the concealed rooms that Anne, her family, and four others used to hide from the Nazis for two years and one month.

I find it hard to visit the Anne Frank House and not envision myself there in 1944 Holland. I imagine the fear they lived in every day, and when the clock tower chimes the hour at Westerkerk, I remember I'm hearing the same bells that gave Anne comfort so many years ago. For me, the most moving part of the house is a spot on the wall where Anne and her sister Margot's heights were marked. My parents did that for me growing up, and I imagine yours did it for you; the only difference is we weren't hiding from Nazis. It's such a subtle and haunting reminder that these were real people trying to keep some familiarity in a world that had gone completely mad.

The Corrie ten Boom House in Haarlem is another moving reminder of Dutch resistance during World War II. The Ten Booms, a Christian family, used a secret room in their house to hide Dutch Jews. The family was eventually discovered and arrested, and Corrie's father and sister both died in concentration camps. But the Nazis never discovered the Jews hidden in their secret room.

Since the end of World War II, the Netherlands has become one of the most secularized countries in the world, and as we left the Anne Frank House, I wondered if the war was to blame. Granted, I have neither the historical nor anthropological training to say what role that terrible war played in the country's shift away from religion, but I suppose it's safe to say the end of World War II did not bring revival. And on a personal level, it's understandable that a person might lose faith after living through five years of occupation by one of the most evil forces the world has ever known; that someone would question God's existence when entire cities like Rotterdam are bombed off the map; that people from a country with a history of wars over Christianity would be tired of both after more than a hundred thousand Dutch Jews were exterminated in concentration camps.

Whether or not World War II accelerated the secularization of the Netherlands, the country is indeed quite secular, with fewer than 20 percent of the population attending church regularly. You, dear reader, may even think of Holland as a modern-day Gomorrah, a Bizzaro America, where sex with prostitutes has replaced baseball as the national pastime and pot brownies are the new apple pie. And while it's true the Netherlands has a relaxed policy toward soft drugs, particularly cannabis, and prostitution is legal and regulated by the government, Americans are actually twice as likely to have tried marijuana than the Dutch, and the average Dutch male is no more likely to have slept with a prostitute than the average American male. That said, most American towns don't have red light districts, or at least not legal ones safe enough for tour groups to walk through, so after Tyler forced us to have dinner at Wagamama, a British-owned Japanese restaurant chain he insisted would change our lives, the four of us went to check out De Wallen, perhaps the most famous red light district in the world.

I'd walked through De Wallen before, on a cold Tuesday morning back in 2010. It's a weird place to see in broad daylight, like walking through a haunted house with the lights on. But we were there on a Friday night this time, and the debauchery was dialed up to eleven. There were people everywhere, and flashing signs in Dutch and English advertised a whole list of things I would never be able to write about in this book. And of course in every direction there were windows full of women in lingerie with red lights shining above them. Some of the women were dancing or trying to get men's attention; others were smoking cigarettes and looking bored.

I cannot begin to tell you how fascinating and sad the red light district is, particularly at night. It's hard to look at, but hard to look away from at the same time. You know stuff like this exists, but to see it in living color is something else altogether. I remember the slack-jawed looks on Bryan and Tyler's faces, which undoubtedly matched my own, while Joseph was unmoved, saying, "It's actually a lot cleaner than Bourbon Street, and at least here superdrunk people aren't screaming at us."

Not for Sale, a nonprofit based in California that fights human trafficking, estimates there are more than twenty-five thousand women working as prostitutes in the Netherlands, many from poor countries in Eastern Europe. Walking through De Wallen, I wondered what the church was doing there, which led me to Lydia, a staff member with Youth with a Mission in Amsterdam who was born in the Netherlands, had spent a dozen years in the American South,[4] and had just recently moved back to Holland.

YWAM Amsterdam has a ministry called the Lighthouse that operates right in the heart of Amsterdam's red light district. Teams gather at the Lighthouse to worship, study the Word of God together, and go on prayer walks throughout the RLD. The girls working in the district are offered healthy soups, coffee and tea, and cookies, and are reminded that Jesus loves them.

"We don't offer the girls a way out," Lydia told me. "We wait for them to ask for a way out. We wait until they start asking questions and show a desire to change and come out of that life. Because we know we're not going to drag anybody out of their old life. We're going to tell them about Jesus and trust that God is powerful enough to move on people's lives and change them."

Talking to Lydia, I wondered not only about reaching those working in the sex trade but about reaching anyone in the everything-goes atmosphere of Amsterdam. "You have to approach people in a different way," she said. "And it's not going to be with rules and regulations. The churches I went to in the States were like, 'Now that you're saved, you've got to stop doing this, this, and this.' You cannot do that here because the Dutch are very proud of their opinions, and if you come in telling them what to do, they're going to be like, 'Who are you?' So we encourage people to draw closer to Jesus, to walk with Jesus, and as God empowers them, you start to hear stories of people's desires changing. They lose their appetite for the world, and even the things that Amsterdam has to offer. So you have to allow the Holy Spirit to change their lives from the inside out, instead of confronting them directly with their sin."

Reinier, Base Leader of YWAM Amsterdam, added, "In the Netherlands I think there is a sense of, 'Christianity? We're beyond

---

4. Lydia attended LSU, though she resisted the urge to chant "Tiger Bait!" at me when I told her I went to Auburn.

that,' or, 'We know better now.' A huge challenge that I see the Christian youth in this country facing is that they want to be relevant to the world, but while doing so, they are often compromising their beliefs. For instance, there's this whole movement that Jesus wasn't actually the Son of God, just a really inspiring man. Or that heaven and hell are not real, just imagery. It's the same 'we know better now' attitude, only the Christian version."

This approach, while pragmatic, also shows a lot of faith. I'm familiar with the "welcome to our church, now here's a list of things you need to stop doing" approach to Christianity that Lydia mentioned, and oftentimes I've wondered if we're just impatient or, worse, if we don't fully trust that God can regenerate a person. I'm not suggesting that we ignore sin, but I like the idea of telling people to draw close to Jesus before we give them the list of do's and don'ts.

■ ■ ■

The next morning, we woke early and ate a vending-machine breakfast in Amsterdam Centraal while waiting on the train that would take us to Maastricht, a Dutch town in the southeast near the border with Belgium.[5] We were going south to meet Becky Castle Miller, whom up until this point we knew only as a reader of Bryan's blog. And despite the fact that the four of us had met each other on the internet, we were all a little nervous about meeting someone else we'd known only online. "Maybe we need a safe word," Tyler said. "In case things get weird and we want to leave." But before we could come up with one, it started snowing outside the train and we all gazed out in childlike wonder, until Joseph remembered that Becky had promised a day of bike riding.

"I think that was a joke," Bryan said. "She's not going to expect us to ride bicycles all day in the snow."

But when we stepped out of Maastricht railway station, there was Becky and two of her three children waiting on bicycles. Introductions

---

5. How near the border? Well, holes eight to twelve at Maastricht International Golf Course are actually in Belgium, so don't forget your passport or you may get detained at the turn.

were made, then Becky told us her husband, Matthew, and their daughter were on their way, and we needed to walk next door to rent our bicycles for the day. So the bike thing wasn't a joke, and we paid ten euros each to rent our rides for the day.

As we were walking out, Matthew and their daughter pulled up, both looking a little worse for wear. They'd had a wreck on the ride over, and I figured if even experienced cyclists were crashing, there was no way all four of us would survive the day on the icy streets of Maastricht.

Before leaving the parking lot, Becky and Matthew went over some basic traffic laws, then gave us a scavenger hunt that listed, among other things:

- Eat Stamppot +4 points
- Ride a bike with grocery bags on the handles while talking on a phone +5 points
- Wash your hands in a sink smaller than your hands +3 points
- Eat herring +5 points (–10 points if you puke)
- Spot a church that's been turned into a sex shop +10 points

And then before we could ask a question, the Miller family took off down the road, leaving the four of us sitting bewildered on our bikes, wishing we'd taken the time to come up with a safe word.

But then we started pedaling through the lovely streets of central Maastricht, and it wasn't that bad. We'd all dressed warmly, except for Bryan and Joseph, who for some reason decided to share a pair of gloves, and honestly, 32 degrees and snowing is a whole lot better than 35 degrees and raining. Within a matter of minutes, we'd gone from dreading the day to come to remembering just how much fun riding a bicycle can be. By the time we reached Vrijthof Square in the center of town, we were all laughing and smiling ear to ear. However, Becky soon found a way to wipe the smiles off our faces.

When we caught up with the Miller family, Becky was walking out of a little market in the town square. In her hands were four slimy herring covered in raw onions. When we spoke via email before the trip, Becky had said she would make the four of us try herring, but I'd pictured us eating little slices on crackers, not holding the entire fish by the tail and dipping it in our mouths.

I'm not sure what happened with the other guys, but I bit down on my herring and immediately regretted every decision I'd made in life that had somehow led to my biting down on a piece of herring in Maastricht. The whole scene is a bit of a blur, but I remember walking around gagging, my fight or flight response converting to spit or swallow. I opted to swallow, but only managed to get it down by holding my nose. Meanwhile, Joseph had just finished his entire herring and was licking his five ungloved fingers when he asked to finish mine.

From there we rode past a beautiful old church that has been converted into a daycare, then another beautiful old church that has been converted into a hotel, before finally stopping at a beautiful old church that has been converted into a bookstore and cafe. There we had cappuccinos and stroopwafels, and Becky taught us to rest our waffles on the brims of our mugs, warming the delicious caramel inside so that the entire concoction melted in your mouth. At this point, Dutch food had broken even, but after later stopping at a frite shop for fries covered in curry, I realized I'd probably starve to death if I lived here.

Over curry fries, Becky told us that in college she'd felt a calling to missions, and how an elder in her church had told her he felt God would speak to her about missions through a dream. "A few days later," she said, "I had this very clear dream that I wrote down. I was in a European city, and I was walking across this open cobblestone square toward this big, old stone church with trees growing in front of it. I went inside the church, and it was empty and dusty and unused, and some young people and I began setting up sound equipment and microphone stands like we were getting ready to have a worship service."

"Ten years later," Becky said, "I reconnected with my former youth pastor, who was now a missionary in the Netherlands. He told me he was moving to a little town in the south and really needed help planting a church, and that we should pray about coming. So we prayed about it, and I began helping as much as I could from a distance, designing their website, among other things, and while I was researching Maastricht,

I came across a photo of Sint-Servaas Basilica in Vrijthof Square, and I had chills, because it was the church from my dreams."

Then as we walked outside, across Vrijthof Square toward the church from Becky's dreams, they told us all of the things that fell together just at the right moment for the family to move to Maastricht in spring 2012. "Our church, Damascus Road International Church, has grown from eight people at the first meeting to more than one hundred and forty on a typical Sunday. We're an international English-speaking fellowship, ministering mostly to expats and students, and people from more than eighty nations have visited the church. We do have plenty of Dutch nationals attending as well, though, because many say they prefer our lively style of worship."

Dutch Catholics form the majority in Maastricht and throughout the southern areas of the Netherlands. An estimated 4.2 million Catholics make up the largest religious group in the Netherlands, though even these numbers have dropped significantly in recent decades. A recent study showed that less than 1.2 percent of the Dutch population attends Sunday Mass. "It's a very unchurched area," Becky told us. "In Maastricht less than 3 percent of the population attend church."

The Millers' friend Michael Krysztofiak, who I think may be the head basketball coach at Duke, told me what it was like to grow up a Protestant in the Dutch south. "There is a lot of Catholicism here," he said, "so for people here, we are weirdos. Some people even think we're a sect. So it's not easy to just start a conversation with a random person. You have to be careful how you approach people here, because Catholicism has such deep roots." Michael told me a big Protestant church in the south consists of a hundred and fifty to two hundred people, but that if you go up north in Holland, there are some megachurches and Protestants aren't as uncommon as they are in the south.

I read a little Dutch history and learned it was after the Calvinist wave of the Protestant reformation that Holland fought an eighty-year war with Spain to gain its independence. Calvinism became a sort of state religion in the Netherlands after independence was won, and religious tolerance was displayed toward most non-Calvinists, which is how Holland became a safe haven for so many Jews. However, the one group this tolerance was not shown to were the Catholics in the south, who were persecuted for centuries. This might explain the cool reception Protestants receive in the south.

■ ■ ■

Later in the afternoon, on our ride out to the old city walls, Joseph crashed off the sidewalk and slid across the icy road, perhaps a result of my cutting him off, but I don't think a Dutch jury would ever convict me. Then near the end of our scavenger hunt, we stopped to take photographs at the Helpoort, the thirteenth-century town gate whose name literally means "Hell's Gate," and I recall thinking they could have probably come up with a better name for the gate to their town. Finally, the nine of us sat around a big table at Bisschopsmolen, a restaurant whose name knocked three kids out of the last Scripps Spelling Bee. There we were introduced to vlaai, a Dutch pie that we all sampled three or four different flavors of, because when your transportation is self-propelled, calories are no longer a concern.

There was more biking and more snow and more sights, then as the sun set, we all stopped at 't Pothuiske, a pub on the Meuse River, to drink a pint and laugh and talk about the day. But all too soon, it was nearing six o'clock and we needed to get back to the station to catch our train, so we walked outside to see Maastricht glowing in an eerie twilight as church bells rang throughout the city. And as we pedaled across the John F. Kennedy Bridge, I stopped to look out over the city and take a mental picture. So much of life goes by in a blur, and I just wanted to pause for ten seconds to make sure I'll always remember the magic I felt that moment in the Netherlands.

■ ■ ■

On Sunday Joseph and I woke early to attend the morning service at Westerkerk while Bryan and Tyler slept in, asking me not to mention that they spent the morning at Starbucks because they are heathens who worship at the throne of caffeinated capitalism. I told them I'd think about it.

Arriving that morning, we passed the snow covered statue of Anne Frank in Westerkerk's courtyard as tourists were already lining up next door to tour her hiding place. A friendly greeter welcomed us at the door underneath the tallest church spire in Amsterdam; the only problem was he welcomed us in Dutch, a language neither of us understands. So like everyone else we met in the Netherlands, he switched to English, speaking it better than either Joseph or me as he said, "You are quite welcome to attend the service this morning, but we must warn you it is entirely in Dutch, and once it begins, you will not be able to leave." Seems the congregation at Westerkerk had had enough of rude tourists disrupting their worship service. Though I suppose locking visitors inside your church is better than locking them out.

Westerkerk is a PKN (Protestantse Kerk in Nederland) church. PKN is the largest Protestant denomination in the Netherlands, with a membership of around 1.8 million. The PKN was founded all the way back before iPhones in 2004, when the Dutch Reformed Church, the Reformed Churches in the Netherlands, and the Evangelical Lutheran Church in the Kingdom of the Netherlands merged. I tell you this only because I think it's cool to see denominations merging, rather than breaking off into even more denominations.

Inside, we sat near the back, listening to the beautiful organ play while worshipers filed in. Our order of worship was, of course, entirely in Dutch, so during the first hymn, I took out my phone and tried to translate. That hymn, at least according to Google, goes something like this:

> Why did I understand your voice?
> Why sir, I need you to go on unaccustomed paths.
> Why have you brought that concern?
> Isn't your blood that grace in me?

Looking back, I think some of it may have been lost in translation.

We didn't understand a word of the sermon, but it used lots of slides of Van Gogh paintings, and after we sang the church blessing and were dismissed, Joseph and I stuck around to enjoy some of the free coffee Westerkerk was handing out. Many of the members thanked us for attending, and when they realized we did not speak Dutch, they became even friendlier, perhaps because we had not tried to leave halfway though the Van Gogh sermon.

As I've noted before, oftentimes when I visit an older church, particularly one like this in a big European city, I get the feeling it's no longer an active church. That it's more of a museum playing church on weekends. But Westerkerk did not feel that way. There was a large crowd that morning, including many families with young children, and I got the feeling it is thriving as well as any church is thriving in Amsterdam.

On our last evening, we spent a couple of cold hours walking around the museum district, Tyler admitting he was only about 80 percent sure which country we'd been in the whole time. "So are we in the Netherlands, or Holland?" We thought about asking a passing cyclist but figured shouting, "Where am I?" would lead them to believe we'd spent a little too much time in a coffee shop. So instead we took the tram back to our hotel one last time. And stepping off at the same tram stop we'd been to at least a dozen times that week, we noticed for the first time red lights on the building just across the canal from us, and in the windows under those red lights were the four most bored prostitutes you can imagine. "Nice job on the hotel," Bryan said. "As if four guys going to Amsterdam doesn't sound fishy enough, now we have to tell our wives we stayed in a red light district."

We stood there for a moment, talking about how strange it must be to grow up in a place where you walk past prostitutes on the way to school, when Joseph said, "Uh, guys, I think they are looking at us." And they were, so not knowing what else to do, the four of us waved at them, and they waved back, and it was all about as awkward as it sounds. Early the next morning, as we left the hotel to catch our train to Brussels, the women were still standing in their windows.

I suppose when I think of the Netherlands now I still think of the seedier parts. It is a place where, even postcard shopping, you run the risk of having disturbing images seared into your retinas. But more than that, I think of the believers we met there, like the folks at the Lighthouse, who are shining the light of Christ into the darkest parts of the world. I pray for them, and I pray for the women in the windows, and I hope by the time I return, some of them have found a way out of that life. I pray for these things, and I pray to never again experience the taste of herring on my tongue.

AUSTRALIA

I come from a land down under,
where beer does flow and men chunder.
—Men at Work, "Down Under"

I'm not convinced God wants people to visit Australia."

"No kidding. It's like he had this big blob of land left when he created the earth and thought, 'I guess I'll just stick this down here on the bottom where no one will notice it.'"

The preceding conversation took place between Russell Clayton, my former college roommate and a reoccurring character in my books, and me, sometime during our six-week flight from Atlanta to Sydney. We didn't mean this as a slight to the wonderful people who live Down Under, it's just that Australia is, geographically speaking, a long freaking way from everything. It feels even farther away when, to use frequent flier miles, you route your inbound flight through Japan, a country that, like all other countries, isn't anywhere near Australia. When we boarded the 747 in Tokyo, we'd already been on a plane more than half a day, and we still had an eight-hour flight full of babies apparently on their way to a screaming convention. And it was on that last leg that we speculated why God had even made Australia to begin with if he was going to make it so hard to get to.

"Maybe God thought kangaroos would look weird anywhere else," I said, doing my best impression of the boxing animal.

"Right," Russell said. "Or maybe if all the land were on the top half of the globe, the earth would be unbalanced and continually flip over."

"Exactly," I said, "it's probably just simple physics." Then after a few seconds of silent confusion, I offered, "Or maybe God came up with the Australian accent first and thought it was too good to waste, so at the last minute he made one more continent."

"It is a good accent," Russell agreed, then countered, "Maybe we misinterpreted the Old Testament, and all of human history was leading up to the Crocodile Dundee films."

I pulled up the Bible app on my phone and after a quick search said, "Proverbs 18:10 says, 'The name of Yahweh is Migdal-Oz.' I think God might actually be Australian."

"Whoa!" Russell said, his mind completely blown. "Why don't they ever tell us this stuff in Sunday school?"

It's possible this bizarre conversation could have been jet-lag related;

however, Russell has a one-year-old daughter, and a few months before this trip, my son, Linus, was born, so at this point in our sleep deprived lives, it's kind of hard for us to tell whether we're jet-lagged or not.

■ ■ ■

We landed in Sydney around 7:00 a.m., and though sleep deprivation has wiped out most of my memories from that morning, the ones I still have paint a picture similar to *Mad Max Beyond Thunderdome*, where two travelers fight each other in a cage, the winner passing through immigration, the loser being put on a flight back to Japan. Russell and I must have won our fights, because soon a bored customs agent was asking whether I was carrying ten thousand dollars or more in cash. "I wish," I said, not even drawing a chuckle, and then we boarded a train to Sydney's Central Railway Station.

Australia is a big country. In terms of square miles, it's the sixth largest country in the world. But no one lives there. Well, twenty-three million people live there (less than the population of Texas, by the way), but at eight people per square mile, it's almost the least densely populated country in the world.[1] Eighty-nine percent of Australians live in urban areas, and all of these urban areas are near the coast, most in fact on the east coast. Which means the vast middle of Australia, known as the Bush, is a barren wasteland governed by boomerang wielding kangaroos. This is probably because the temperatures in the vast middle part occasionally reach 120°F, and one time stayed above 100°F for 160 consecutive days.

The Dutch discovered Australia in the sixteenth century, which must have come as a surprise to the one million indigenous Australians already living there. Then in 1770, Captain James Cook claimed Australia for Great Britain, back in the days when you could just sail around the world claiming things like that. After losing Georgia in the Revolutionary War, the British government needed a new penal colony, so they began sending

1. Greenland is the least densely populated country. There you encounter .07 percent of a human every square mile, which sounds gross.

convicts to their Australian colonies of Norfolk Island, Van Diemen's Land, Queensland, and New South Wales. These days Australia is a federal parliamentary constitutional monarchy, so they elect their own government, but the Queen of England still gets to be on their coins.

I've read about thirsty travelers in the desert mistaking a mirage for water, and I feared perhaps our empty stomachs had tricked our minds into seeing that red and green Krispy Kreme sign in Central Station. Oh, but it was real, and we ordered three donuts and a coffee each, and the bill came to twenty-four dollars, which I thought had to be a mirage as well, but according to my credit card statement, it too was very real.

"Maybe this is why they asked if we'd brought ten thousand dollars with us," Russell said, and I began to fear he was right.

Our hotel was a short walk away, but this didn't really matter because they told us it would be six hours before we could go to our room. So we took turns washing off as best we could in the lobby restroom sink, then walked down George Street in the direction of Sydney Harbor.

I wasn't overly impressed with Sydney at first. When you leave Atlanta and spend nearly twenty-four hours in an airplane, you don't want to end up somewhere that doesn't look all that different from Atlanta. Admittedly, at this point our cognitive abilities were only a step above zombie—I may have even bit a man thinking he was a sandwich—but still, it wasn't love at first sight. But then we reached Circular Quay,[2] with the famed Sydney Opera House to our right and the majestic Harbor Bridge ahead on our left, and I was tempted to call Tricia to tell her to pack all of our things and meet me in Sydney.

We rested in the grass near the harbor for a few hours, watching battleships and fighter jets pass by because Sydney was being attacked by New Zealand. Okay, not really; we were there for the Australian Royal Navy's Fleet Review Week, along with about a billion other people. Then we met up with Kelly Seo, a friend of Kelsey Beckman, the native Kansan I met in Barcelona all the way back in the Spain chapter.

---

2. Australians pronounce words with very little regard to phonics. I suppose they do this so they can pick out foreigners trying to fake Australian accents. The phrase "quay, by the way" doesn't rhyme in Australia, because quay is pronounced like "key."

Kelly is Korean Australian, something my jet-lagged mind had trouble comprehending. Not that I didn't think there were Australians of Korean descent; it's just I wasn't really expecting to meet a girl who looks very Korean, yet talks very much like Nicole Kidman.

Kelly took us on a walk through the Rocks, the oldest section of Sydney and the site of Australia's first European settlement in 1788, and there we took a table outside the Australian Hotel, a 189-year-old pub where we sat in the sun sipping Dirty Granny Ciders, because Kelly told us only Americans think Foster's is Australian for beer.

"You've got to try the 'roo," Kelly said, pointing to the Pepper Kangaroo Pizza on the menu, "and the crocodile." So we ordered a pizza with half kangaroo and half crocodile, along with a pepperoni, just in case. I could take or leave the man-eating reptile topping, but I've been craving marsupial ever since I got home. Now every time I call Domino's, I ask if they have kangaroo, but as of last week, chicken is still about the most exotic thing they serve.

As we were leaving, Kelly invited us to her church on Sunday afternoon, and while we were writing down directions, a cavalcade of police cars, sirens blaring, came roaring past our table and Kelly shouted, "It's Prince Harry!" And sure enough, there in the back of a limousine was the ginger-headed Prince of Wales, in town to inspect the Royal Fleet, and party hard, probably.

That evening after a quick nap, we walked back down to the harbor for the massive fleet inspection fireworks extravaganza, though Kelly had warned us it would be "damn crowded with people and portaloos." She was right; we never even got close enough for a clear view of the harbor and were instead reduced to watching the tops of the fireworks explode over the tops of downtown skyscrapers. So we ate dinner at a chicken finger place on George Street, sitting next to this tattooed Aussie guy who watched us nervously for a few minutes before asking, "Are you guys cops?"

"No," Russell said, "we're Americans."

"Oh, man," the tatted dude said with what looked like relief, "I can't wait to go to America one day. The girls there have amazing accents."

At this Russell and I exchanged bewildered glances, but I suppose everyone's accent sounds exotic to someone.

We bid our strange new friend a good evening and walked back to the hotel, where our receptionist said, "We wanted to remind our guests that daylight saving time begins tomorrow, so you will want to set your clocks ahead one hour tonight." This isn't exactly what two jet-lagged and weary travelers wanted to hear. Stupid southern hemisphere.

■ ■ ■

Throughout the course of researching for this book, I'd had the opportunity to attend a Hillsong church in no less than five cities, but I held out, knowing that later I'd be in Sydney and could visit the mother ship. We woke up early to make the second of five Sunday services at Hillsong's Hills Campus in Baulkham Hills, a suburb twenty miles outside of Sydney. To get there, we took the train to Parramatta, then waited with about two dozen others for the free bus service provided by the church. Thirty minutes later, we arrived.

The husband and wife team of Brian and Bobbie Houston began Hillsong Church in 1983. Back then the church was called Hills Christian Life Centre and had a congregation of less than fifty people. Thirty years later, more than thirty thousand people attend a Hillsong service each week, either at one of the main four Australian locations, one of the dozen extensions across Sydney, or one of the growing number of international locations, including Moscow, Barcelona, Los Angeles, and New York.

Hillsong's main campus is located in the Norwest Business Park, and you drive through a maze of soulless office buildings before you spot a sign with Hillsong's logo written in familiar script. Then you see a large green lawn leading up to the Hillsong Convention Center, a glass and metal structure that could be mistaken for an NBA arena, except for the massive white letters above the entrance saying, "Jesus, Hope for Humanity." Our bus turned down the long drive and parked between the convention center and a smaller modern chapel that also hosts Sunday services.

Our service was in the convention center, and Russell and I walked in past two Disney-esque mascots that I hoped were part of the children's ministry, then past the large Hillsong store selling CDs, DVDs, mugs, and T-shirts, and down into the massive auditorium, taking two seats that would have been near half-court had this actually been an NBA arena. A few minutes later, a video began to play as the lights went down to reveal hundreds of candles lighting the stage. And as the images flashed faster and the music pulsated louder, the arena rose to its feet and began to worship.

At this point I'm going to assume even if you have no idea what Hillsong is, you've probably heard some of their music. They are responsible for "Shout to the Lord," the "Hey Jude" of contemporary Christian music, along with about half the other songs you probably sing on Sunday morning. Hillsong has released more than fifty albums since 1992 and has sold more than twelve million records. Their first youth album, *We Are Young and Free*, had just released[3] when we were in town and was already climbing the mainstream charts in Australia and the United States.

That morning the worship band consisted of a lead singer, a few guitarists, a bassist or two, a girl shredding on the violin, a drummer, a few singers, a choir of about twenty-five children, some guy who appeared to be in charge of making sure the twenty-five children were constantly jumping up and down, a percussionist, and some keyboardists. I can only assume an oboe, a hurdy-gurdy, and a glass harmonica were being played just off stage.

Their first song was upbeat and fun, and many of the youth down front were hopping and dancing with their hands in the air. I remember feeling a bit of a children's show vibe during the service, like I was watching the Wiggles in concert. But in Hillsong's defense, we were there on a special Sunday. I'm not sure the twenty-five jumping kids are typically on stage, and later the children of the church did perform their annual skit, a Noah and the ark presentation whose set design

3. Or is it dropped?

rivaled Russell Crowe's big screen version. Then later we were treated to a live performance of the 2013 Kidsong Big Word Memory Verse song, and though I tried to fight it, that song wormed its way into my brain and stayed there for the better part of the week.[4]

Pastor Brian and Pastor Bobbie were in New York City that morning for Hillsong Conference USA at Radio City Music Hall, so Robert Madu, a pastor from Trinity Church near Dallas who'd spent the last few days speaking at the Hillsong Youth Encounter Conference, preached in our service, and he was funnier than most of the stand-up comedians I've seen.

As a first time guest at Hillsong, it was going to be hard not to find myself at times sitting back and enjoying the show. I'm an old soul, I realize that, and I think highly rehearsed, flawlessly executed worship services like the one we attended that morning always weird me out a bit at first. But that's my problem, not Hillsong's. And while Hillsong has certainly become a brand name, it's a brand name that gets people's attention. Check out some videos from Hillsong Stockholm or Hillsong Copenhagen and you'll see vibrant, thriving churches in two countries where only about 20 percent of the population even believe in God. There's nothing wrong with people showing up for the spectacle but staying for Jesus. Hillsong is doing big things around the world, and the church particularly appeals to young people, which at thirty-six years old I am not, even if I still wear my hat backward. (Kids still wear their hats backward, right? Get off my lawn!)

After lunch at Nando's, a South African restaurant chain, where we ate spicy chicken in silence while staring intently at Russell's phone anticipating updates on the Auburn-Ole Miss game from his wife, Alicia, we took the train to Strathfield and met up with Kelly and her friend Jean.

"Russell and Chad," Jean said with a laugh after Kelly introduced us. "Those are such American names."

"Thank you," we said, not sure it was meant as a compliment.

---

4. *http://www.youtube.com/watch?v=4OZwtzA8Bys*. One listen and you'll be singing it the rest of the day, whether you want to or not.

Before church we stopped at Sweet Cafe, a neighborhood coffee shop where Kelly taught us that you have to say "long black" if you want a normal American cup of coffee. Then the four of us walked down to her church, the Rock Church, which sits hidden among rows of houses on a residential street.

Church began, and after an acoustic worship set, a man in a suit walked up on stage and was introduced as Herbert Edwards, an Aboriginal missionary Rock Church has been supporting for almost twenty years. Herbert shared part of his testimony and gave an update on his work among the Aborigines in the Bush. Kelly told me later it is easier for Korean Australians to reach the indigenous population than it is for Caucasian Australians, because of the bad history.[5]

Kelly's friend David agreed. "I've been involved in missions groups here in Australia and around the world, and all the groups I've been around have mentioned how it has become more difficult for Caucasians to go into certain parts of the world, like the Middle East or North Korea, because in many countries there is a negative stereotype associated with Caucasians, whereas people from Asian backgrounds generally do not share that stereotype."

After the service, we hung around and talked to Kelly and her friends Daniel and Tabitha. I asked Kelly what it is like being a Christian in Australia and she said, "I definitely don't feel like I'm in the majority. Most of my Christian friends are from church, and a lot of my friends from university are atheist or have strong liberal views. But saying that, I don't think it's socially unacceptable to be a Christian here."

Kelly certainly had a different college experience than Russell and I. A few months before this trip, Auburn had been named the most conservative and the eighth most Christian college in the United States. When we told Kelly this, she said, "There's a neighborhood near here called Auburn, but it's very dodgy."

"How dodgy can it be?" I asked. "You guys don't even have guns."

"Quite dodgy," Kelly said.

---

5. This bad history includes the introduction of smallpox and the forced removal of around fifty thousand Aboriginal children from their families, among other things.

This led to the inevitable conversation about how dangerous America is, and I began to realize a lot of people outside of America think the typical American day isn't all that different from a Michael Bay film. I wanted to argue that Australia isn't exactly the safest place on earth, since almost every animal on the continent is venomous, but I also wanted Kelly and her friends to think that at least once a week I calmly walk away while a car explodes behind me, so I let it go.

Before we left the church, Kelly took the time to pray for us, then she drove us back to Strathfield Station, and after giving us goodbye hugs, she handed us both a jar of vegemite and said, "Australians put this on bread. The key is to use a little vegemite and *a lot* of butter." We thanked her, hesitantly, then sat and waited on the next train back to Sydney.

"Do you notice anything odd?" Russell asked, after the train screeched to a halt in front of us.

"You mean that there appears to be only teenage girls on the train?"

We boarded and took the only two empty seats in a cabin full of young girls, many of them wearing the same T-shirt, all of them talking excitedly about something. I glanced over at the girl next to me and saw in her hands a program with a photo of five young men, then noticed the same five young men were on her T-shirt, and everyone else's T-shirts. Curiosity finally got the better of me, so I asked, "Is everyone on this train coming back from a One Direction concert?"

"Yes!" she yelled, and giggling broke out in the rest of the cabin. Not knowing what else to say, I asked if it had been a good show. "Oh, don't act like you weren't there," shouted the girl in front of us, then the giggling and screaming resumed. This was pretty much the worst train ride I'd ever been on.

That evening at dinner, we watched the National Rugby League Grand Final between the Sydney Roosters and the Manly Sea Eagles.[6] I once sat by an Australian on a plane and he spent the better part of the flight explaining to me why rugby is better than American football, or

---

6. Manly is the name of the town, not an adjective describing the Sea Eagles themselves, but seeing that they are big men who crash into each other without helmets, I suppose it works both ways.

gridiron, as he called it. His argument boiled down to a sport not really being a sport unless every player ended the game with a broken nose. After the match, which the Roosters won by breaking all their noses first, we saw a massive brawl on George Street between opposing fans. Russell and I watched for a minute or two, but when one of the contestants looked our way, we took off running toward our hotel. We both knew there are lots of scary animals in Australia, but we'd never even considered death by rugby hooligan.

The next day, Russell and I took a train, then a bus, to Bondi Beach, the most famous beach in Australia. It was a brilliant spring day, and a kind stranger told Russell, who is perhaps the palest person I know, "You're gonna want some sunscreen, mate." Sunscreen applied, the two of us stood on Campbell Parade, looking down the hill toward the incredible crescent moon shaped beach.

We walked up the beach toward the cliffs on the Ben Buckler coastline, and just as we passed the North Bondi Surf Life Saving Club, a group of volunteer lifeguards whose services I hoped we wouldn't need, the sky, in what seemed like a matter of seconds, turned black and started spraying everyone with cold stinging rain. But no sooner had we taken cover in a coffee shop, the clouds were gone and the sun shone as brightly as ever. This only drove home the notion that danger is always just around the corner in Australia.

Next time you are bored and surfing the web, pull up the top ten most deadly snakes in the world. More than half the entries will begin with "found in Australia." There is a snake in Australia called the death adder, and it's not even the deadliest snake in the country! And out in the waters off northern Australia is Belcher's sea snake, one of the most venomous snakes in the world. A few milligrams of its venom can kill one thousand people.

But it's not only snakes. Australia has ants that attack you, ticks that can paralyze you, eighteen-foot saltwater crocodiles that can swallow you, twenty-six-foot great white sharks that can swallow the saltwater crocodile that just swallowed you, and something called a box jellyfish, ten feet of translucent terror that, despite feeding on a diet of small fish,

God decided to pack with enough venom to kill sixty adult humans. I don't think anyone would have complained had Noah decided to leave a few of these off the ark.

After a ten-second conversation on whether we should rent surfboards ("Want to rent surfboards?" "Box jellyfish." "Oh, right."), we walked back to the south end of Bondi Beach for lunch at a place called Bondi Icebergs.

Bondi Icebergs is a club with a fifty-meter Olympic-size pool that appears to rise naturally out of the rocky coastline on the southern end of Bondi Beach. Since 1929 local lifeguards have maintained their fitness during winter months by swimming laps here. Above the pool sits a four-story building with a gym, yoga studio, and the Bondi Icebergs Bistro, where you have to be a member to eat. Thankfully the only step to becoming a member is presenting your driver's license to the woman at the door, and soon Russell and I were enjoying fish and chips and beer during the most scenic and delicious lunch either of us could remember, high above the death adders and saltwater crocs on the Bondi Icebergs balcony. Membership has its privileges.

After lunch we decided to try the Bondi to Coogee walk, a three mile trek that takes you past one gorgeous beach after another, each of them broken up by breathtaking cliffs and rock formations. The weather grew more spectacular each minute, and there were people everywhere. The ocean was full of surfers showing total disregard for the sharks and jellyfish below them. The beaches were full of sunbathers and kids playing soccer, oblivious to the saltwater crocodiles that at any moment could drag them to a gruesome demise. And the grassy parks were dotted with picnickers and frolicking children seemingly unaware that death adders were slithering beneath their feet. And when you see everyone else relaxing and enjoying themselves, it's kind of hard not to relax and enjoy yourself as well, particularly when you're walking along the most scenic stretch of ocean you've ever seen.

But I suppose that's one of the things you learn while traveling; everybody is dealing with their own scary stuff. Some cities have hurricanes, while others have wildfires, some sit on fault lines, and others have yeti attacks, maybe. Yet when I asked Kelly if a box jellyfish had ever killed someone she knew, she looked at me like I was Mel Gibson crazy. I guess what I'm trying to say is we shouldn't let fear of sharks or tsunamis or terrorists or jellyfish keep us from seeing the world. I'm not saying we should be careless out there, but if we're spending the majority of our time reading about what can go wrong in the country we want to visit, we are doing it wrong.

■ ■ ■

It's easy to think of Christianity in Australia beginning and ending with Hillsong, but that would be a mistake. Hillsong belongs to the Assemblies of God in Australia (AOG), a Pentecostal denomination that has more than 225,000 adherents across Australia, which seems like a lot, until you consider that that makes up only 1.7 percent of the more than thirteen million Christians in Australia. Roman Catholics make up the largest group of Christians in Australia, with more than 40 percent of the population, while the Anglican Church comes in second, accounting for a little less than 30 percent.

Kelly's friend David introduced me to Stephen, an assistant minister at Randwick Presbyterian just south of Sydney, and he told me of the Christian Church in Australia: "It is growing, and it is culturally very diverse, especially in the major cities. The next generation is looking to churches that are proclaiming Jesus as Lord and Savior. The externals don't matter much anymore. People seem happy to join a church whether it's in a new building or an old church building, as long as Jesus is being proclaimed and they can be part of the mission."

However, Stephen's comments contradicted a conversation I had later with a pastor from western Australia, who referred to Australia as post-Christian and told me church growth statistics Down Under paint a sad picture.

For me these two conversations encapsulated an inherent weakness of this book—namely that I would never be able to provide more than a snapshot of Christian life in each country, and even that snapshot would be a bit blurry. In the end I can tell you only what I saw and report the opinions of people I spoke to, opinions that sometimes varied greatly. Even opinions on Hillsong were all over the map, but I imagine the opinions on your local megachurch are too. And in a way, hearing such contrasting views on Australia only strengthened the feeling that Christianity there isn't all that different from back home. Sydney actually could have been Atlanta or another large US city with booming megachurches and smaller congregations that are either struggling or thriving, depending on who you ask. It felt familiar because we've influenced them, but you can't discount the influence they've had on us. Speaking of Brian and Bobbie Houston, Ed Stetzer, president of Lifeway Research, said, "I'd guess that globally, they'd be in the top ten influential evangelicals in the English-speaking world."

That evening, we tried to attend a prayer service in one of the old churches Stephen mentioned, St. James' King Street, a nearly two-hundred-year-old Anglican church across from Queen's Square.[7] I say we tried to attend, because when we arrived, the church was dark and obviously closed.

"Where is everyone?" Russell asked.

"Beats me," I said. "Maybe they all forgot to spring forward for daylight saving time."

But then I pulled up the church's website on my phone and realized that it was I, not every member of St. James', who was mistaken about the service time. I also noticed that once a month St. James' has a children's service in their Crypt, which might be the creepiest thing I've ever heard.

I thought I'd be more upset about missing the service at St. James', because when you fly around the world for the sole purpose of attending a few church services, you kind of hate to miss one. But Australia is a laid-back place, and after a few days, that laid-back attitude apparently had rubbed off on me.

---

7. St. James' was designed by Francis Greenway, a British architect who was sentenced to death for forgery but later had his sentence commuted to fourteen years in Sydney. Best punishment ever.

I remember thinking the relaxed vibe would probably make being a Christian in Australia easier than in some overly stressed country. But Kelly's friend David told me, "One of the biggest difficulties growing up as a believer in Australia is the laid-back, easygoing attitude we've adopted. This cripples many believers from really hungering for God's presence and his Word and experiencing him on a deeper level."

David's friend Peter, a pastor at Inner West Baptist Church in Sydney, echoed his friend's thoughts, telling me, "We have a saying here, 'She'll be right, mate,' which means 'don't worry about it.' This laid-back attitude often hinders decision making."

After striking out with the Protestants, Russell and I tried to salvage the evening and hurried down the street toward the Metropolitan Cathedral of St. Mary, a large Gothic revival cathedral whose massive twin spires we'd seen in the distance from the train earlier in the day. But as soon as we arrived, the evening Mass was coming to an end and parishioners were emptying into the street. So I shrugged and told Russell, "She'll be right, mate," then we walked through the Royal Botanical Gardens and out onto a peninsula where we watched the sun set brilliantly into the harbor behind the famed opera house. This, we figured happily, would serve as our religious experience for the day.

■ ■ ■

A few days later, after riding more ferries and walking on more beaches and meeting more of the nicest people in the world, Russell and I had our last meal in Australia on the roof of the Glenmore, a restaurant in the Rocks that offers spectacular views of Sydney Harbor and the Opera House. And over juicy burgers, it dawned on me that I'd now been to six of the seven continents and had probably seen more in my last two years than I'd seen in the previous thirty-four.

"No, you can't go to Antarctica," Tricia said when I called home later that evening. "What would you even write about, Christian culture among penguins?"

"There is a Russian Orthodox church in Antarctica," I said.

“Oh, so you want to get scolded for crossing your legs on every continent?”

“Not really.”

“I didn’t think so. Just hurry back, okay?”

“I will,” I said. “I just need to stop by China on the way home.”

CHINA

But if you go carrying pictures of
Chairman Mao,
you ain't gonna make it with anyone
anyhow.

—The Beatles, "Revolution"

Typically you don't swing by China on your way home from Australia the way you'd swing by the pharmacy on your way home from work, because China, like everywhere else in the world, is nowhere near Australia. But it made more sense than flying all the way home across the Pacific and then flying all the way back, so while Russell was on his way back to his wife and baby in Florida, I was on a plane to Hong Kong, where I met my high school friend and fellow Auburn Tiger Jeremy.

Upon arrival at Hong Kong International Airport, you are confronted with a sign that tells you to remove any headwear to facilitate infrared temperature detection. Then you pass through an Orwellian human quarantine scanner under the watchful eyes of officials in a nearby booth. This freaked me out and probably raised my body temperature a degree or two, but I made it through to immigration, wondering what they'd have done to me if I'd actually had the flu. Then at passport control, which I assumed would be equally intense, my officer's cell phone rang to the tune of Kylie Minogue's "Can't Get You out of My Head." He silenced it before giving me a sheepish grin and quickly stamping my passport. Ten minutes in and China was exactly like I thought it would be, and exactly unlike I thought it would be.

Hong Kong is a good way to ease into China. It became a British colony after the end of the First Opium War (which apparently was a real thing) in 1842, and remained as such until 1997, when the United Kingdom transferred sovereignty back to China. Since then Hong Kong has operated under China's "one country, two systems" policy, which gives it a high degree of autonomy in everything but foreign relations and military defense. For instance, a travel visa is required for a US citizen to visit mainland China, but not Hong Kong.

Jeremy and I met in the arrivals hall and took the MTR Airport Express train to Kowloon Station near our hotel. Our absurdly modern room was on the fifty-third floor, and with the press of a button, the automated window shades slowly opened to reveal a breathtaking view of Victoria Harbor and Hong Kong Island. I conservatively estimate we hit the window button forty-three times before forcing ourselves to get out and explore the bustling city.

More than seven million people live in Hong Kong, making it a pretty crowded place. Its 17,024 citizens per square mile seemed particularly absurd coming from Australia's eight per square mile.[1] We hailed one of the dozens of red taxis waiting outside our hotel, and as our driver navigated the crazy traffic, we took in the sights and sounds of the city.

Hong Kong is the most vertical city on the planet. It ranks first in the world in both skyscrapers and high-rise buildings, meaning your neck is kind of sore after visiting. The Hong Kong skyline would be impressive if it were in the middle of Kansas, but when you combine it with Victoria Harbor and the surrounding mountains, you have one of the most beautiful cities in the world. And there is only one place to see it all from, Victoria Peak.

Victoria Peak is truly breathtaking. The only place I've been that compares is Corcovado in Rio de Janeiro, except in Hong Kong there isn't a nine-story Jesus looking over your shoulder.[2] There could be, I suppose. Religious freedom is a fundamental right guaranteed to all Hong Kong people. One of the first things we saw when arriving in Kowloon was a massive sign covering the side of a high-rise building that said, "Jesus is Lord." Rick Warren's Saddleback Church even has a Hong Kong location. But despite these freedoms, Hong Kong is one of the least religious places in the world, with a recent Gallup poll stating that 64 percent of Hong Kong residents do not follow any religion.

The cool breezes atop Victoria Peak were a welcome relief after the stuffy humid air below, so Jeremy and I stayed up there until well after dark before riding the tram down, then taking the Star Ferry[3] back across Victoria Harbor to the Temple Street Market, a night market

---

1. Maybe you're thinking this has to be the most crowded place on earth, but you'd be wrong. Manila in the Philippines has a population density of 111,002 per square mile, making Hong Kong look like a barren wasteland in comparison.

2. There is, however, an eleven-story Buddha called the Tian Tan Buddha (aka Big Buddha), located on Lantau Island near Hong Kong's airport.

3. The Society of American Travel Writers once named the Star Ferry the most exciting ferry in the world. I'm still not exactly sure what makes the Star Ferry more exciting than any other ferry; perhaps kung fu fighting breaks out from time to time, because our ride, while lovely, wasn't what I'd call exciting.

where you can buy anything from blue jeans to fresh squid straight from the tank. Replacing the lens cap I'd lost on Victoria Peak was not a problem; though, regrettably, I passed on buying one of the many bizarre Chinese-English decorative signs for sale, particularly the one that read, "You are my love angel, don't treat me like a potato."

■ ■ ■

The next day, we flew from Hong Kong to Beijing, a three-hour flight that shattered more of my preconceived notions about China. Before this trip, when I thought of China, I thought of a terrified populace shuffling through the streets, their heads down, their eyes averted, lest they make eye contact with some secret policeman who could send them to the salt mines. This is actually the way I think of any Communist country, a byproduct, I suppose, of growing up in the United States in the 1980s. It's a stereotype, of course, but I did think the Chinese were probably a lot more likely to follow the rules than someone in the United States. I was wrong.

"Did she answer that?" Jeremy asked, referring to the woman in the row behind us whose phone rang during our takeoff roll.

"Oh yeah," I said, though in the woman's defense, she'd kept the conversation short.

I'd estimate the flight attendants had to ask no less than seven people to take their seats during our rather steep ascent, had to scold dozens of passengers for not wearing their seatbelts during the flight, and had one very animated conversation with a man who took his son to the restroom two minutes before landing. And as we prepared to touch down, I turned to Jeremy and asked, "What's the over/under on the number of people who try to get their luggage out before we've come to a complete stop?"

"How many people are on the plane?" Jeremy said. "Because they are all going to do that."

Then we touched down smoothly, and every seatbelt in the plane unbuckled with one loud click, and by the time we reached our gate, no fewer than ten passengers had been told to return to their seats.

Immigration at Beijing Capital International Airport moved swiftly, but this only managed to bottleneck everyone at a luggage scanning station everyone had to pass through before leaving the airport. Well, everyone except for one woman who got in a heated argument with one of the men scanning our luggage, then proceeded to walk around the entire enterprise. When this happens in American airports, it's the lead story on the evening news. Here the man shrugged and turned to the next person in line.

We figured flights and airport rules were one thing, but once we got outside in Beijing, things would be more orderly, more controlled. Again we were wrong. Outside the airport, there was no shortage of unmarked taxis trying to swindle tourists by charging ten times the going rate. One almost got us, but instead we hopped in a marked yellow and green taxi, immediately regretting it. Several times during the white-knuckle drive to our hotel, I had to shut my eyes. But it wasn't just our driver; it seemed every car on the road was racing toward some unknown finish line, many of them swerving in and out of orange cones that were clearly marking road construction. I just knew at any moment we were going to fly off the end of an unfinished bridge, but instead we actually made it to our hotel, or a few hundred yards from it. The driver made us walk the last part without really explaining why.

Lying in bed that night, fighting the urge to eat the ten dollar Pringles from the minibar, I recalled a conversation I'd had a few weeks before with Jonathan Smyth, a fellow Auburn graduate who has spent a lot of time in China working with the English Language Institute. Jonathan warned me that the reality of China would likely contrast sharply with my assumptions. "Every time you think you've got China pinned down," he told me, "you'll see something and say, 'Wait a minute, that's not what I thought China was.'"

Jonathan told me the name of a church I should attend while in Beijing, and even that flew in the face of what I thought I knew about China. I'd heard about international congregations where only internationals were permitted to attend, and I'd heard about the underground church that met in secret and was under constant threat from the government, but this church appeared to be made up entirely of Chinese nationals and obviously was not hiding from the government, since their meeting place and time were listed right there on their website.

I asked Jonathan about this, and he said, "The church I emailed you about, Haidian Church, is a Three-Self church, part of the Three-Self Patriotic Movement. Basically, these are government-registered churches that abide by the three principles of self-governance, self-support, and self-propagation. This assures the government that there is no foreign influence on these churches."[4]

"So I guess the government controls the message these churches can preach?"

"People always ask me that," Jonathan said, "because they think surely these churches are just a mouthpiece for the Communist Party. But you can look at the statement of faith for the Three-Self Churches. They took the whole Bible, not just parts approved by the government, they took the Apostles' Creed, and they took the Nicene Creed, and they combined it all to build their statement of faith. So it's not very different from your church in Auburn. You've got very evangelical, mission-minded churches."

"I'm confused—so why are there underground house churches again?"

"A lot of it has to do with control," Jonathan said. "House churches would say they don't want to submit their church to an atheist authority, where the Three-Self Church would say that the Bible says to submit to the authority God has put over you. So you find these illegal house churches in rural areas."

And just when China was beginning to make a little sense, Jonathan added, "In cities in the last ten to fifteen years, we've seen the emergence of the urban church, and the difference between it and the house church is that the urban church is made up of influential leaders from the business sector, from the government, from medicine—it's made

---

4. The Three-Self Movement also assured the government that churches would be patriotic to the People's Republic of China. Patriotic churches seem much stranger when they are being patriotic to a country that is not your own.

up of the movers and shakers of the city who happen to be believers. So the reason we put them in their own category is because while they are unregistered and technically illegal, they are so influential and powerful that they are virtually untouchable. A lot of the people attending these churches are the same people responsible for enforcing the rules that would cause their churches to cease to exist."

"Everything I hear about China only manages to confuse me more," I said.

Jonathan laughed and said, "Everything you hear about China is probably true somewhere in China, and this speaks to the diversity of China in so many ways. Is there persecution? Yes, somewhere. Is there religious freedom? Yes, somewhere. Is there a one child policy? Yes, somewhere, and somewhere else there is freedom to have multiple children. It's mind-boggling because things that make sense one day in China make no sense the next."

■ ■ ■

The next morning, Jeremy and I went for a stroll through Beijing, which, at least on that morning, wasn't nearly as smoggy as advertised.[5] Not long after leaving the hotel, we were approached by a young Chinese woman who seemed really interested in practicing her English. So we talked to her about Yao Ming, who she said is now too fat to jump, and then we had the following conversation on China's one child policy.

"So in China you are allowed to have only one child?" I asked.

"Yes," she said, "but if you do not live in the city and you have a girl, you can try again to have a boy. And if the mother and father have no siblings, they can have two children together."

"It's a little different in the US," Jeremy said, and our new friend said, "Yes, I have read about your Octopus Mother who gives birth to eight babies at a time."

Jeremy and I laughed out loud, and I said, "She only did that once,

5. It got worse. Our last day there, you could almost taste the air. Some scientists believe a quarter of the smog in California actually comes from China. Worst export ever.

but we have another lady who's had nineteen babies. She has a TV show." I'm fairly certain our new friend thought I was lying.

After a couple of hours of aimlessly wandering, we found ourselves in Tiananmen Square, which, at four and a half times the size of Millennium Park in Chicago, is huge. We entered the square from the north, near the Tiananmen Gate to the Forbidden City, and strolled south toward the Mausoleum of Mao Zedong. This was the second chance I'd had to view an embalmed Communist, and the second time I'd passed.

"I wonder where the guy stopped the tank?" I asked.

"Yeah, there's probably not a marker for that," Jeremy said.

The guy and the tank were from the Tiananmen Square Protests of 1989, also known as the June Fourth Incident, when the Chinese government broke up seven weeks of student led protests for democratic reform by declaring martial law in Beijing and killing hundreds (if not thousands) of unarmed civilians with assault rifles and tanks. It was during this madness that an unidentified Chinese man, in what became one of the most iconic photos of the last century, stood and blocked a column of Chinese tanks from advancing through the square.

There was no marker, but there were police everywhere, along with tall lampposts covered in futuristic security cameras. *This* was more what I thought China would feel like, but even so there were smiling tourists everywhere, many of them posing for photographs in front of the beautiful flower displays left over from National Day on October 1. And I think the strangest thing were small groups of Chinese soldiers marching in formation throughout the square, and how Chinese tourists were never in a particular hurry to get out of their way. Occasionally soldiers would just weave their way through a crowd, instead of expecting the crowd to part. I wouldn't call it civil disobedience, maybe civil indifference, but either way it was nothing like I'd expected.

We had a difficult time with taxi drivers in Beijing. Even when we were able to show them the location we wanted to go written in Chinese, accompanied with a map in Chinese, they would sometimes shake their heads and drive off. It took four tries to find a taxi willing and able to drive us out to a neighborhood near the 2008 Olympic Park, where we met Philip Selway, a Canadian expat living in China whom a friend back home had hooked us up with.[6]

Jeremy and I sat with Philip outside a small cafe in north Beijing, sipping hot tea and asking him about the drivers in China.

"I've lived here for more than a decade," he said, "and I've never seen anyone get pulled over for a traffic violation. Police cars are always riding around with their lights on, but they don't pull you over. I can't imagine how bad you'd have to be driving to actually get a ticket in Beijing."

"So what is it exactly that you do here in Beijing?" I asked.

"Oh, I spend about half of each day in prayer," Philip said, then he took a sip of his tea, giving Jeremy and me a chance to exchange befuddled glances. "But I also mentor two dozen home church pastors here. I meet with them and pray with them and assist them in any way I legally can. But I do not do anything illegal that will get me thrown out of the country, which is why I do not attend their churches."

"So that's what the government would do?" Jeremy asked. "Throw you out of the country?"

"Oh, yes," Philip said. "I wouldn't be tortured, if that's what you are getting at. They're not going to throw a westerner in jail for proselytizing. They just send you home and tell you that you cannot come back. The pastors I mentor, though, most of them have been tortured at one point. But nothing too bad."

"Wait, the torture wasn't too bad?"

"Right. My pastors tell me, and they believe this, that in China today there is just enough persecution.[7] You see, there are no casual Christians here. So the fear is that when the persecution goes away entirely, so will the passion and growth they are seeing in the underground church."

"And what's interesting," he continued, "is on a local level, many

---

6. Not really. I mean we really met with someone, but they weren't Canadian, and they asked for me not to reveal their personal information. Philip Selway is a pseudonym, and also the drummer for Radiohead. We did not meet the drummer for Radiohead, I'm almost positive.

7. They should put this on T-shirts. "China: Just Enough Persecution."

officials have no problem at all with the underground church. My pastors tell me they've even worked with policemen, because the police know if the youth of their district are in church, it makes their jobs that much easier."

"But why don't they go to the sanctioned churches? A friend told me they are gospel-driven. Is that not the case?"

"Oh, no, he is right. You said you're going to Haidian Church on Sunday right? Well trust me, you will hear the gospel of Christ there. There are great things happening in both churches."

"So why do these house churches risk it, if they could just go to places like Haidian?"

"Because they believe their government is the Antichrist."

Noticing the quick glance Jeremy and I exchanged, Philip explained that in the underground church, there is a belief that the Chinese Communist Party is the red dragon referred to in Revelation 12, also known as Satan, and that membership in the CCP is the mark of the beast foretold in Scripture. I googled this when we got home and found websites verifying exactly what Philip said, but fair warning, when you search on "China + Antichrist," you can end up in some rather strange corners of the internet.

Philip pointed to the shops around us and said, "China, as you now know, is not North Korea. When I first arrived, it was more totalitarian, but things have changed drastically in China since I've been here, and they are changing more and more every day. The Chinese government doesn't have a problem with Christianity. What the Chinese government has a problem with is large groups of people meeting without their knowing about it. If three thousand photographers wanted to get together without the government's knowledge, that's going to be a problem."

After Philip left the cafe, Jeremy and I took a stroll through the Olympic Park, past the Beijing National Stadium, affectionately known as the Bird's Nest, and the sparkling Water Cube. We ended up in a mall that evening, shopping at a Nike Store. And while we were laughing at the large selection of Charles Barkley Dream Team jerseys on sale,

Robin Thicke's "Blurred Lines" thumped through the speakers overhead. This was example number 354 of how China is nothing like I thought it would be.

■ ■ ■

Later in the week, we took a guided tour of the Mutianyu section of the Great Wall of China, and Amanda, our tour guide, spent most of the drive out recounting the wall's history. But the history lesson consisted mostly of a bunch of dynasties neither Jeremy nor I could keep straight in our heads, so we interrupted and asked Amanda to show us on her phone how Chinese people send text messages. Then later, after noticing the fat smiling Buddha on the dashboard, Jeremy asked Amanda about religion in China.

"In China we are very free," she said. "You can be Christian, Jewish, Muslim, whatever you like. In China many people practice Daoism and Buddhism," then pointing toward the dashboard, she said, "This is Budai. Legend says he was very poor, but very happy. He was always laughing, and he was very fat." Then turning and pointing to Jeremy, she said, "You! You are big and happy like the Budai." This cost her some tip money from Jeremy, but I gave her double because I laughed like the Budai for five minutes.

We rode a gondola up to the Great Wall and Amanda pointed toward a watchtower in the distance. "You should walk to there and back," she said. "Some people you see have gone farther, but that part of the wall is closed. Many tourists practice civil disobedience at this place on the wall."

"These mountains are so steep," Jeremy said. "Wouldn't they be enough to protect you from Mongols?"

"You have never met a Mongol," Amanda replied.

Walking up and down the Great Wall was a workout neither of us really wanted. At each watchtower, we stopped, both of us laboring to breathe. In the end, we did go past the "do not go past here" sign, which was there only because the wall is crumbling and it looks rather easy to fall to your death. Then we walked back down to Amanda, who was shocked by the color of Jeremy's face. "Why is your face so red like you drank all the wine?" This time I was too tired to laugh.

After the wall, we went back to Beijing to tour the Forbidden City, walking through the Tiananmen Gate to the Imperial City, passing underneath the famous portrait of Chairman Mao.

Jeremy and I made it a point to refer to everything inside the Forbidden City as forbidden. We asked Amanda if we could use the forbidden restroom, and if there'd be a chance to buy forbidden souvenirs, and if we could stop for some forbidden ice cream. She never smiled, however, and I can only assume our jokes were lost in translation.

■ ■ ■

On Sunday, after having three separate members of the hotel staff try to tell our taxi driver where exactly we wanted to go, we arrived at Haidian Christian Church, part of the Three-Self Patriotic Movement. Haidian Church appears to be constructed entirely of massive white beams, giving it the sleek modern look of many new churches in America. But unlike some of the new churches back home that almost try not to look like a church, Haidian has a forty-foot cross standing in the entryway, with the words "Christian Church" emblazoned in tall red letters, high above for all to see.

When we arrived, the fourth worship service of the morning was beginning, and outside, members of the church were conducting free eye exams for locals. I peeked inside the church to see a standing-room-only crowd, then Jeremy and I walked around back to the 3W Coffee Shop to meet Jonathan Smyth's friends Jessie and Levi, a young Chinese couple who run Haidian's college ministry.

We sat down and ordered cappuccinos, our mugs adorned with slightly misquoted lines from *Forrest Gump*: life *was* like a box of chocolates. A few minutes later, Jessie and Levi arrived and we all sat at a large table looking out on the church grounds. Jessie asked about our time in China.

"I wasn't expecting so much rule breaking," I said. "When we learn about China back home, we're taught you guys have this very strict government, and I assumed everyone would obey every rule down to the letter. I kind of figured no tag had ever been removed from a pillow in China."

They laughed and Levi said, "Oh, no, Chinese people do not like to follow the rules."

"I also didn't really expect to see a church this crowded. I looked in the sanctuary before we came here and there were people standing in the back."

"Look over there," Jessie said, pointing at a doorway with people spilling out onto the sidewalk. "It's the overflow room, where people can watch the service when the sanctuary is full."

"Have you eaten well?" Levi asked.

"No," Jeremy said. "Last night we had eyeball soup at one of those restaurants with Bruce Lee on the logo."

"Not Bruce Lee!" Levi said with a laugh. "No one eats at Bruce Lee; it is so gross!"

This was not entirely true; there were plenty of people eating at Bruce Lee the night before, but I'm starting to think we'd discovered China's answer to Taco Bell.

Jonathan told me that Jessie had spoken at a Passion Conference in Atlanta a few years earlier, so I asked her impressions of the United States.

"There were so many churches," she said. "Churches on every road, and so many different kinds. Here there is only the Christian Church, Protestant and Catholic. I did not know about all the denominations until I went to America."

I told them I could walk to at least ten churches from my house in Auburn, and they couldn't believe it.

"We visited Auburn," Jessie said. "Jonathan took us on our way to his house in Montgomery. He showed us your famous toilet paper trees, but told us later that a crazy man had poisoned them."

"It's a sordid tale," I said, then we walked over to the sanctuary where Haidian's English service was about to begin. There were a few westerners in the service, but the crowd was mostly Chinese, and a band opened with Hillsong's "Shout to the Lord." Later we sang "Amazing Grace" and "How Great Thou Art," and then the sermon, as predicted, was as gospel-centered as anything you'd hear in the Bible Belt.

I couldn't wrap my brain around what I was experiencing and what I'd expected to experience. Surely there was some government intervention. "Levi, do you guys have to attend Haidian because you live in this district?"

"Oh, no," he said. "You can attend wherever you want, but it's just easier to attend the church closest to you. Haidian even has about fifty satellite services in the district if you don't live close to the main building."

Back in the coffee shop after the service, I asked Jessie and Levi if they'd grown up in Christian homes.

"Levi did," Jessie said.

"My parents were members of a Three-Self church in the small town where I grew up," Levi added.

"How small?" I asked.

"Six hundred thousand,"[8] he said, and I nearly spit my coffee across the table.

"My family were not Christians," Jessie continued, "but growing up, I would watch American movies and television shows, and people were always going to church to pray, or getting married inside these beautiful churches. I decided when I came to Beijing for college, I would find one of these churches to see if they truly exist. At college, some friends introduced me to a Christian guy who said he would take me to his church, and one Sunday morning we went."

"Wait, so you're telling me Hollywood movies are the reason you wanted to attend a church?"

"Yes," Jessie said. "But then we got there and people were talking about all these crazy things and I thought, 'Oh, this is just a club, and

8. China has 160 cities with a population of one million or more. The United States, by comparison, has nine.

you have to say you believe crazy things to get in.' I told my friend this on the walk home, but he argued with me. He said he truly believed the things he said, but I did not believe him. We argued until curfew that night, and I went to bed furious with him. But when I woke up the next morning, everything was different. I called my friend and told him that I believed and I wanted to be baptized."

Jessie's story was a beautiful reminder of how far God will go to draw a soul to him. I think sometimes as Christians we put a lot of pressure on ourselves, as if the eloquence of our words will ultimately determine whether a person follows Jesus. Don't get me wrong, we have a responsibility to tell people about our Savior, but it's great to know in the end that if God wants someone, he'll use any means necessary to get them, even romantic comedies.

Levi had to work that afternoon, telling us, "There was a holiday during the week, so we must make it up on the weekend."

"Wait, you have to make up holidays on the weekend?"

"Yes, this is why every Chinese person you've met this week has been so angry."

We laughed and said our goodbyes, and Jeremy and I hailed a taxi.

"Airport?" we asked, and the driver's head nodded in the affirmative. It may be the only English word they all know. And after another white-knuckle ride, we sat eating some delicious airport dumplings, reflecting on the trip. In the West, we often hear about the growth in China's underground church, which is awesome, but I was equally impressed with what I saw in the Three-Self Church, because before this trip, when I thought of Christians in China, I certainly didn't think of a large sanctuary crowded with Chinese nationals lifting their hands and singing "Amazing Grace." You've probably heard missionaries or friends who went on short missions trips say something like, "God is doing great things in China." Well, China is a big place, and I'm not sure anyone can really speak with any authority on the country as a whole. I know the tiny sliver I saw certainly prohibits me from doing so. But God is at work in China. I caught a glimpse of it, and the people I spoke to there have glimpsed it too. So when we say things like, "God is doing great things in China," I think it's just a natural reaction to seeing any movement of God up close, because everything God does is great. I won't pretend that there isn't persecution, that house church pastors aren't imprisoned, and that believers haven't been tortured. The country has some serious problems, but China isn't what I thought it would be, and it probably isn't what you think it is either, and I hope someday you have the opportunity to see that for yourself. Jeremy and I both wanted to stay and see more ourselves, but it was time to go, and two hours later, we boarded our plane and watched as Beijing disappeared into the smog.

ISRAEL

O come, O come, Emmanuel,
and ransom captive Israel.

—"O Come, O Come, Emmanuel,"
Trans. Neale and Coffin

Just think," my friend Billy Wilson said as our overstuffed British Airways flight from Heathrow taxied to its gate at Ben Gurion Airport near the Tel Aviv suburb of Lod, "Jesus and his disciples used to fly in and out of this very airport."

I laughed, thankful to be on the ground after two long and exhausting flights and a half day layover in cold and soggy London.

I'm almost positive Billy was joking—he *has* been to seminary, so maybe he knows something I don't—but even so there was some truth to what he said. Everywhere you go in Israel the history overwhelms you. Peter never flew British Airways, but he did heal a paralyzed man in Lod,[1] probably right behind the Domino's Pizza.

Coffee and muffins preceded a thirty-minute taxi ride to our hotel just across Herbert Samuel Avenue from the Jerusalem Beach in Tel Aviv. In the hotel parking lot, there were hundreds of discarded flyers for a strip club featuring attractive women in various stages of undress. Our driver pointed them out and said, "Welcome to the Holy Land."

We tried to check in, but it was early, 8:00 a.m. or so, and I suppose it goes without saying that our room was not ready and would not be ready for some time. The hotel was nice enough to let us shower off in their gym, though, and while I was waiting on Billy in the lobby, I noticed one of the elevators opening every so often without anyone getting on or off. The receptionist must have noticed my confusion, because she said, "It is a Shabbat elevator."

"Come again?"

"Some believe Jewish law prohibits operating electrical devices on Shabbat, the Sabbath. From sundown Friday until sundown today, this elevator continuously opens on every floor, so people can ride the elevator without breaking Jewish law."[2]

Billy and I'd only had trace amounts of sleep in the last forty hours, but we resisted the urge to take naps in the hotel lobby and instead filled

1. Acts 9:34.

2. Jews can also hire someone known as a Shabbos goy, a non-Jew who can perform certain types of work for Jews on Shabbat. Teenage Elvis Presley was once a Shabbos goy for his neighbors in Memphis. Just a hunka hunka Shabbos goy.

up on some free coffee and stepped outside onto the Tayelet, a promenade that runs along Tel Aviv's Mediterranean shore. Before this trip, when I heard the name Tel Aviv, the first thing that came to mind was the 1991 Gulf War and how the city was a favorite target of Saddam Hussein's Scud missiles. Since then there have been numerous suicide bombings in the city, and just twelve months before our visit, Tel Aviv was again targeted by rockets, this time coming from the Gaza Strip. And I suppose when you know only the scary things about a place, it's hard not to imagine the most nervous city ever, where women carry gas masks in their purses and everyone walks at a brisk pace, not wanting to be stuck outside when the air raid sirens sound. Yeah, Tel Aviv is nothing like that.

Tel Aviv is a beach town, and when you live in a beach town, I think it's hard not to enjoy life. That morning the sun was shining bright and people were out everywhere, running, biking, swimming, rollerblading, and walking dogs. This did not jibe well with my preconceived notions of Tel Aviv. I wanted to grab someone and say, "There are people forty miles from here who want to blow this entire city into the sea. How can you rollerskate at a time like this?" But Tel Aviv is not a nervous city. With its beautiful people and swanky hotels and tall palm trees, it could be any Mediterranean city, or Miami's South Beach for that matter.[3]

■ ■ ■

We think of Israel today as a Jewish state, and with Jews making up more than 75 percent of the population, it is. But there are also a significant number of Arabs living in Israel, around 1.4 million, who were residents of Mandatory Palestine and remained there after the establishment of the State of Israel following the 1948 Arab-Israeli War. Christians make up only about 2 percent of the Israeli population, around a hundred and fifty thousand, and the majority of those Christians are Arabs. This is a little confusing to my American brain, because while we love and support Israel, we're a little less loving and supportive of Arab people.

---

3. We spoke to some Israelis with friends in Be'er Sheva, near the Gaza Strip, and during rocket attacks, they simply go into a downstairs safe room and watch DVDs and play PlayStation until the attack ends. It's like a slumber party with gas masks.

Before our trip, I'd read a book called *When Your Neighbor Is the Savior* by Botrus Mansour, an Arab-Israeli Christian and director of the Nazareth Baptist School, and later I spoke to Botrus and asked him about life as an Arab Christian in Israel. "Being an Arab Christian brings mixed feelings," Botrus told me. "First it brings pride because of our history. There were Arab Christians since the day of Pentecost. Through the years, Arab Christians have been holding on to the faith of their fathers despite persecution. But on the other hand, it brings frustration because belonging to the Arab people in general comes with challenges. Jews see us only as Arabs; our Christianity is put aside. Our relationship with the Jews is shadowed by the Arab-Israeli conflict and is full of bigotry, prejudice, discrimination, and stereotypes."

I asked Botrus whether he felt discrimination as a Christian in Israel, and he said, "I don't feel discrimination in Israel as a Christian but as an Arab. What applies to Arab Muslims applies to me too."

Nazareth, the hometown of Jesus, is now the largest Arab city in Israel, and nearly 70 percent of the population in Nazareth is Muslim. I asked Botrus about the significance of being a Christian in the hometown of Christ, and he said, "It is a big privilege as well as a huge responsibility. The hometown of Jesus is a special place, and followers in his hometown should be a lighthouse and a real testimony. Nazareth has a Muslim majority, so as the living stones[4] of Nazareth, we have to shine in a bright way."

We were in Israel for only a few days and didn't have a chance to travel up north to Nazareth to worship with Botrus and his fellow Arab Baptists, which is a shame because I've always wanted to pull into Nazareth feeling like half past dead. So instead I searched for a congregation in Tel Aviv that we could visit. Finding one wasn't easy, though, as Christians make up only about 1 percent of the population in Israel's second most populous city. But then I stumbled across the website of Adonai Roi, a Messianic Jewish congregation, and I was intrigued.

Not knowing exactly what Messianic Jews are, I clicked the link on

4. 1 Peter 2:5.

the Adonai Roi website that said, "What Are Messianic Jews?" and it took me to a page that said, "Coming Soon." I wasn't sure whether this was a prophecy or if their website needed updating; however, I later learned that Messianic Jews basically combine Christian theology with Jewish practice, making them, in overly simplistic terms, Jews who believe Jesus Christ is the Messiah. I was also pleased to see that even though Adonai Roi's services are in Hebrew, headphones are provided for those wishing to hear the English translation.

While looking to purchase property of their own, Adonai Roi were currently meeting at the Beit Immanuel Guest House, a three-story guesthouse just a few blocks from the sea that is owned by another Messianic congregation. Billy and I arrived early because we'd spent the last three hours wandering Tel Aviv and wanted to sit down, but I'd forgotten the church was meeting in a hostel, and we stood outside for a while, not sure we were in the right place.

However, once we saw other people carrying Bibles go inside, we followed suit and took a couple of chairs in a large downstairs room where a worship band that looked and sounded like any other college age worship band (except they had members playing a flute and harp, and they were singing in Hebrew) was practicing their set list, and we listened to them for about an hour before the service finally began. Worship that morning was lively, with the crowd of about sixty on their feet, and the children of the church down front waving large flags to the music.

From my seat in the corner, I could see only about half of the projector's screen behind the band, but this didn't matter since everything appeared to be in Hebrew. I'd asked Billy on the flight over whether he recalled much Hebrew from seminary, and he'd told me it was very rusty, but when I looked over during the first song, I saw him singing loudly in Hebrew. I honestly thought I was witnessing some dramatic movement of the Holy Spirit that was enabling Billy to worship in an ancient language, but later he told me the side of the screen I couldn't see had an English transliteration of the lyrics.

After the music, which went on for a while, there was an Old Testament reading, and then some more music, and then a woman stood up, commandeered the microphone, and began sharing with the congregation a dream she'd had.

"This just took an interesting turn," I whispered to Billy, who raised his eyebrows and smiled.

I don't recall much about the woman's dream, but at her request, we soon broke up into groups of three or four to pray for Israel. After that a few others took their turn addressing the congregation, then we sang a little more, and finally a guest preacher from Jerusalem began to deliver the morning's message.

About an hour into the message, my eyelids grew pretty heavy, and I noticed that every now and then Billy's head nodded violently. I want to make sure you know this had nothing to do with the morning's sermon but had everything to do with our approaching forty-eight hours without sleep, and perhaps a little to do with the service approaching three hours. So I nodded toward the back door, and Billy and I slipped out into the sunny Tel Aviv afternoon.

■ ■ ■

On Sunday morning, a crowded bus picked us up at our hotel and drove us to a massive parking lot, where dozens of other crowded buses were loading and unloading hundreds of tourists all in preparation for a day of Holy Land exploration. Now, I don't actually have the numbers to back this up, but I'm going to say Israel has the highest number of tour buses per capita in the world. In fact I'm pretty sure every Israeli owns a tour bus. Tourism, as you've gathered, is quite big here. Three and a half million tourists visit the Holy Land each year, which is impressive when you consider that most people don't visit areas of the world they think are synonymous with rocket attacks. But perhaps when you hear people say things like, "I just want to see the Holy Land before I die," they're actually expecting to die on the trip.

I was less concerned about rocket attacks than about contracting Jerusalem syndrome, a mental phenomenon where otherwise normal people become psychotic after the overwhelming religious experience that is Jerusalem. It's a real thing; you can look it up.

You realize just how small a country Israel is when you bus the forty miles from Tel Aviv to Jerusalem. It's not much bigger than New Jersey—after ninety minutes in traffic, you've driven all the way across it. Along Highway 1, our guide pointed out abandoned military vehicles from the 1948 Arab-Israeli War and informed us that until 1967, Jordan controlled parts of this road and Israelis were forced to take a detour on their way to Jerusalem.[5]

After stopping at a hotel to drop off some of our bus mates and pick up a few more, we drove to the top of Mt. Scopus and were presented with a breathtaking panoramic view of Jerusalem. I could have stayed up there for hours looking out on the ancient city, but a man in our group nearly lost his wallet to a pickpocket and the tour moved on. But before descending into the city, we drove around the backside of Mt. Scopus to look out on the Judaean Desert, and oh, my word, it was the most desolate thing I've ever seen in my life. I suppose deserts by definition are desolate, but still, I wouldn't want to spend forty seconds out there, forget forty days and forty nights without food and water.

As I mentioned earlier, the history in Israel is overwhelming, but particularly in Jerusalem. "On your right you will see the Mount of Olives, where Jesus ascended into heaven. Now if you'll look to your left, you will see the garden of Gethsemane, where Jesus was betrayed and arrested." Hearing this I scrambled to take photographs out the window of our bus, realizing later I'd managed to snap only a couple of blurry shots of other tour buses passing us on the road.

Our group entered the Old City through the Zion Gate, weaving our way through the Jewish Quarter, down ancient streets and over a section of Hezekiah's Broad Wall—a wall built 2,700 years ago. Then we turned a corner and found ourselves looking across an open plaza at the Western Wall, the gleaming Dome of the Rock high above to the left, the Al-Aqsa Mosque, also known as the Farthest Mosque, above on the right.

---

5. In 1967 Israel fought a six-day war, the aptly named Six-Day War, in which they defeated Egypt, Jordan, Syria, and Iraq and took control of the Gaza Strip, the West Bank (including the old city of Jerusalem), the Golan Heights, and the Sinai Peninsula. A great deal of the news you hear today about Israel and Palestine is a direct result of this war; unfortunately, I don't really have the space to explain it in a footnote.

The Western Wall is what remains of the Second Temple, the one destroyed by Rome in 70 AD. As you may recall from Sunday school, the mountain where the temple resided is called the Temple Mount, and it's the place where many biblical scholars believe Abraham bound Isaac, intent on sacrificing his son to God. At the center of this mountain, or hill, really, is a massive rock called the Foundation Stone. According to the Jewish faith, it was from this stone that the world was created, and the Holy of Holies in the temple once sat right on top of it. This makes the Foundation Stone the holiest site in Judaism, which is a bit of a problem, since it's now covered by a giant Muslim shrine called the Dome of the Rock.

You've seen the Dome of the Rock; it's the massive golden dome that dominates almost every photograph of Jerusalem. Completed in 691 AD, it sits upon the Foundation Stone, the stone that, according to Islamic scholars, is the spot from which Muhammad ascended to heaven. Muslims also believe Abraham bound his son here, intent on sacrificing him to God; however, they believe that son was Ishmael, not Isaac.

There were hundreds of Jews praying at the Western Wall when we arrived, the men on the left, women on the right. Jews pray here because they believe all of God's blessings spring from the Holy of Holies, and according to tradition, the Western Wall was the closest wall to it.[6] For this reason, pilgrims also stick more than one million prayer notes into the wall each year. Shmuel Rabinovitch, Rabbi of the Western Wall, receives hundreds of notes each year in the mail from Jews who cannot make it to Jerusalem, addressed simply to "God, Jerusalem." And thanks to modern technology, Jews around the world don't even have to use a stamp, as local rabbis now accept notes via fax and email.

From the Western Wall, we entered the Muslim Quarter of the Old City and began to retrace the Via Dolorosa, which is believed to be the path on which Christ carried his cross to his crucifixion. Our guide informed us that this current route was established in the 1700s,

---

6. Jews are allowed to visit the Temple Mount now, though they are not permitted to pray there. Many Jews refuse to visit, however, not wanting to accidentally walk over the Holy of Holies.

replacing previous routes once used by pilgrims. Hearing this I kind of stopped paying attention and assumed the current route was probably agreed upon by merchants who wanted to make sure the maximum number of pilgrims passed by their souvenir shops while retracing the steps of Christ's suffering.

At the third station of the cross, our guide showed us the supposed handprint of Jesus on the wall of a thirteenth century Franciscan chapel. "This stone is believed to have been touched by Jesus Christ when he fell for the first time on his way to Golgotha."

Sure, I thought to myself, while examining the T-shirts at the shop next door. One featured a fighter jet and said, "Don't worry, America, Israel has your back." Another, aimed at southerners, I suppose, simply said, "Shalom, Y'all." Then I started to take a photograph of one that looks like a Google search on the word Israel, and below it says, "Did you mean PALESTINE?"

"No photographs!" snapped the man behind the shop counter, so I turned and took a photo of Christ's supposed handprint instead.

The call to prayer echoed through the air as we left the Muslim Quarter and entered the Christian Quarter, eventually finding ourselves on the rooftop courtyard of the Church of the Holy Sepulchre, the church that is believed to contain both Golgotha and the empty tomb of Jesus.

Five groups of Christians manage the church—Roman Catholic, Greek Orthodox, Armenian Orthodox, Coptic Orthodox, and Syrian Orthodox—and they don't always get along. In fact their disputes sometimes become violent. This is why the Nuseibehs, a Muslim family, have kept the keys and opened the doors to the church every morning since 1191 AD.

"The Roman Emperor Constantine sent Helena, his mother, to the Holy Land in the year 326 to search for holy relics," our guide told us outside the door to the church. "There was a temple standing here dedicated to Venus, and Helena ordered it destroyed. Underneath she found Golgotha, the tomb of Christ, and three crosses. They were able to determine which was the cross of Christ by having a sick man touch all three; the one that healed him was the cross of Christ." I rolled my eyes and we stepped inside the church.

How the Church of the Holy Sepulchre could actually contain Golgotha made no sense until we stepped inside and I realized that a large part of the church is built around the rocky hill. We climbed stairs with hundreds of other pilgrims, making our way to the top, where everyone patiently waited their turn to kneel and crawl inside an incredibly ornate altar and touch the top of Calvary.

Well, some people waited patiently, but the throngs behind me began pushing and shoving, eventually pinning me against a shrine of the Virgin Mary. I wanted to scream, "This rock has been here for two thousand years; it will still be here in ten minutes if you'll just wait your turn." But it wouldn't have mattered because I could see in their eyes they'd all contracted Jerusalem syndrome. Calvary was only a few feet away, but this dark crowded space was my worst nightmare come true, and I decided I didn't really want to touch it anyway.

"I touched Calvary," Billy said, after I'd fought my way through the crowd and found him waiting near the staircase. "Did you not touch it?"

"No," I said. "I'm going to demand a refund."

From there our group walked down the stairs, past a man in a Red Sox cap kneeling to kiss the Stone of Anointing and around to the Aedicule, the chapel that contains the tomb of Christ. Unfortunately the Aedicule had a line longer than Space Mountain's, so our group took some photos of the outside rotunda, then went to eat falafel for lunch.

I should note here that there are alternate locations for Calvary and the tomb. Perhaps the most famous was proposed by Charles George Gordon in 1882 and is referred to by Protestants as the Garden Tomb. Gordon believed the cliff above the Garden Tomb looks like a skull, which I guess it sort of does. There are other suggested sites as well, and they all have their arguments, and they all have their arguments against the other sites, and in the end I had a hard time getting too worked up over any of it.

After lunch our group loaded up the bus and drove through the Israeli–West Bank barrier, a controversial wall that when completed will stretch 430 miles and separate Israel from the West Bank. The section of the wall we passed through was twenty-six feet tall and made of concrete, and we had to wait only a matter of minutes at the military checkpoint, which is quite a contrast to West Bank Palestinians, who are often delayed hours.

We were on our way to the little town of Bethlehem, which is now a Palestinian city of about twenty-five thousand. We parked near the John the Baptist Souvenir Shop, and our new Palestinian guide (our old guide was Israeli and had to leave us at the border) walked us down a busy street to the Church of the Nativity, a beautiful fifteen-hundred-year-old basilica built on top of what is believed to be the cave Jesus was born in.[7]

The line to the Grotto of the Nativity was stretching outside the door, so our new guide took us in another door and had hushed conversations with men working at the church. He then came back to us and said, "The Greek Orthodox are about to have a short service; after that you will be able to enter the grotto without a wait." Billy and I looked at each other with a shrug and sat down to wait, and immediately an Orthodox priest grabbed my shoulder and scolded me for crossing my legs. I wanted to protest, but I've been to Russia, and I should have known better.

From my place in line, I couldn't see the Orthodox service, but as it finished and incense drifted through the church, our group was whisked to the front of the line in groups of four, leaving me alone in my chair. Our guide, who seemed frustrated that we had an odd number, put me in a separate line and said, "When they ask if you are with a group, you must say no, otherwise you and I will both be in serious trouble."

"You want me to lie in the Church of the Nativity."

"I want you to say no if they ask if you are with a group. Look around—technically you are no longer with the group."

---

7. Helena also found this site on her trip to the Holy Land, and like the Church of the Holy Sepulchre, the Church of the Nativity is controlled by multiple denominations that don't always get along. Palestinian police have been called to break up brawls between monks on several occasions.

So I lied my way down into the Grotto of the Nativity, which is another crowded space where people wait with various degrees of patience to kneel in front of an ornate altar and touch a spot on the floor. When I heard my pastor, Rusty Hutson, describe his visit to the Grotto of the Nativity, it almost sounded like a life-changing religious experience. And down in the cave, pilgrims were singing and praying in different languages, which I suppose is a beautiful reminder of how the baby born here two thousand years ago changed the world. However, my claustrophobia and I lasted only about a minute before I climbed out of the grotto and went outside for some fresh air.

Finally, before the prerequisite stop at "my cousin's gift shop; he will give you lowest prices in Bethlehem, guaranteed," we went to something called the Milk Grotto. This is a cave near the Church of the Nativity in, I suppose, the general direction of Egypt, where Mary was supposed to have breastfed the baby Jesus on their way to exile. There's even a white spot on the stone where some of Mary's milk was reported to have dropped. I may or may not have laughed out loud when this story was told.

I'm not sure why all the holy sites we experienced that day rang a little hollow with me. When I got home, a friend asked me about Jerusalem, and I remember the funny look he gave me when I said it reminded me of Pigeon Forge. What I meant is that it was very touristy, and I hadn't really expected that. The explanations used to justify the guesswork on the locations bothered me too, and at one point I said to Billy, "This should be called the Church of the Nativity, Maybe." But Easter and Christmas are commercialized, and the dates we celebrate them not only are wrong, we know they are wrong, yet I'm still able to find meaning in them. And I suppose I've found some meaning in the Holy Land sites after the fact, because there is something beautiful about centuries of pilgrims returning to the same spots to celebrate Christ's birth or crucifixion. I just wish those places could be more pure, and a little less touristy, but then I guess it's naive to expect tourist attractions not to become touristy.

So if you're like me, you might not feel the sacredness others talk about in the Church of the Nativity or the Church of the Holy Sepulchre, but that doesn't mean there aren't quiet, poignant moments to experience in the Holy Land. For me, simply driving south from Jerusalem and seeing the little town of Bethlehem on a distant hill was a reminder of the humble way our Savior entered the world. I stood in awe before the Western Wall, knowing it was part of the same temple where twelve-year-old Jesus sat among the religious teachers and later drove out the money changers. And walking through the markets of Jerusalem, it wasn't hard to imagine Christ carrying his cross down the same narrow cobblestone streets, while the crowds mocked and cursed him. In the end I didn't need to look at a bronze star on the ground marking the exact location of some event in biblical history. Just being in the vicinity was enough for me.

The next morning, our bus picked us up outside our Jerusalem hotel and took us down Highway 1, through the West Bank checkpoint, and into the Judaean Desert, where we quickly descended below sea level, our ears popping the whole way. Again, the history was too much to properly comprehend.

"On your right you will see the well of the Good Samaritan. To your left is the ancient city of Jericho. Up ahead are the caves David hid in while running from King Saul."

We spent the morning at Masada, King Herod's mountaintop palace that overlooks the Dead Sea, then after lunch visited a Dead Sea resort, where we rented towels, covered ourselves in black mud, then gingerly stepped across the rocky beach into one of the saltiest bodies of water on earth.

Floating in the Dead Sea was fantastic. I imagine it's something close to what astronauts experience, if spacewalking is anything like covering yourself in mud and splashing around with a bunch of half-naked strangers on the Israeli-Jordanian border. Just make sure not to wash your bathing suit with the rest of your clothes when you get back, unless of course you prefer all your clothes to smell like rotten eggs.

■ ■ ■

On our last day in Israel, we decided to rent bikes and just hang out in Tel Aviv. We were riding down the sunny promenade, stopping at a red light, when another bike came zipping in between us. "Only tourists stop at red lights," the rider said. Then looking back at us as he rode away, he shouted, "Welcome to the Middle East!"

We spent that morning exploring the ancient port of Jaffa, where Peter resurrected the widow Tabitha and where Jonah went to catch a boat instead of going to Nineveh. Then after a delicious lunch, we rode over to the Dugit Messianic Outreach Centre, where our friends from Adonai Roi offer free coffee and tell other Israelis about Jesus the Messiah.

Simon, who'd provided the Old Testament reading at the service the week before, welcomed us, and we apologized for leaving the service early, citing our jet lag and lack of sleep.

"Oh, there's no need to apologize," Simon said. "Our pastor is trying to get the church on Swiss time, but he was out of town last week, so things ran a little long."

Over coffee Simon explained that within Israel, Messianic Jews are called Yehudim Meshichim, a direct translation. The Hebrew word for Christian is *Notzrim* and translates to something like "followers of the man from Nazareth." Simon said, "We as Messianic Jews don't use the term Christian in defining ourselves for several reasons. One being that the words Notzrim and Christian bring, to the Jewish mind, a history of persecution—the Crusades, the Inquisition, the Holocaust—and not love, salvation, or redemption."

Simon told us Messianic congregations range from ultra-orthodox to more charismatic, and when I asked him what it is like in Israel for Messianic Jews, he said, "There are not many Messianic Jews in Israel, about 0.2 percent of the population, so many people do not know what a Messianic Jew is. Legally we are not considered a religion but a cult. Some Jews couldn't care less about us and say, 'Whatever works for you,' while others say, 'You are damned and trying to steal and corrupt the souls of Jews.' Many find our faith fascinating but believe they could never accept Yeshua, or Jesus, because they think it means converting and giving up their Judaism. We do not believe one is converted. Yeshua came to the Jews first and brought salvation to the rest of the world."

Simon continued, "Some Arab Christians hate us simply because we are Jewish, but some born-again believers are wonderful friends of ours. We will worship together, pray for one another, speak at each other's congregations, and even go on outreach together. For the most part there is little persecution in Tel Aviv. I wouldn't go as far as to say we are accepted, but more tolerated and ignored."

It was strange to think we were in the birthplace of Christianity, the epicenter from where our faith spread throughout the world, and yet two thousand years later, Christians make up only a small percentage of the population. I suppose I knew this before the trip, but seeing it really opened my eyes, because there are churches all over the country, and yet the Christian community has dwindled to a marginalized majority of Arab Christians, Orthodox communities best known for fighting over holy sites, and a small group of Jesus-loving Jews that most of the country doesn't even know exists. We thanked Simon for his time and told him we'd be praying for his ministry, and then we went to enjoy some delicious Mediterranean cuisine while overlooking the Mediterranean itself.

I loved my time in Israel, even if throughout this chapter I sound frustrated with how touristy parts of the country are. It's all about expectations, I suppose. Before the trip, I probably pictured myself at Golgotha or the Garden Tomb, head bowed in deep prayer, when in reality I bowed my head only to use it as a battering ram to get away from those places. There were moments, though, when I was aware I was walking in the footsteps of my Savior, and if I ever return to Israel, I will know to savor those even more.

The next morning, I was back at Ben Gurion Airport, going through the same intense security screening Jesus and the apostles went through two thousand years ago, before boarding my plane to India.

INDIA

From Bombay to Bangalore,
all the Hindus know the score.

—Jesus Loves You,
"Bow Down Mister"

"You must look at the eyebrows."

Vari, the tour guide my friend Matthew Richter and I hired to show us around Mumbai for the day, must have seen the concerned look we exchanged when a sad woman holding an even sadder baby began knocking on the back window of our car. The baby was no older than my son, and the lady was giving him water from a bottle, and the whole scene made me incredibly sad, and I wanted to take out my wallet and give her every rupee I had, but our guide wouldn't allow it.

"You must look at the eyebrows," she said again. So I did, and I must admit, the woman's eyebrows were perfect. "These women, they are everywhere, and they drug these babies and take turns standing in the road with them, begging for money. But at night, these women will be dancing in the clubs. They have lots of money. They all work for the mafia."

The mafia part seemed like a stretch, but I'd been in India only a few hours and could hardly call myself an expert on the organized crime scene there. I also considered that perhaps between all of these women, one of them might own a pair of tweezers, but figured if you're poor enough to be feeding your baby water in the middle of Mumbai traffic, you probably aren't overly concerned with a flawlessly plucked brow. But scam or not, it was a sad introduction to India.

■ ■ ■

I'd flown to Mumbai's Chhatrapati[1] Shivaji International Airport from Tel Aviv, landing around 1:30 a.m., and after quickly passing through customs, I met Richter, who'd landed only minutes earlier.

Our hotel offered airport transfers for less than six bucks, and after paying four times that for donuts in Sydney, I couldn't help but marvel at how far a dollar goes in India. Walking out of the airport, we were greeted by a man holding a sign that read, "Mr. Chad Gibbs and Mr. Richter Guest Gibbs."

"I'm Chad Gibbs," I said. "And this is Richter Guest Gibbs."

---

1. The second *h* is silent, probably.

"Father and son?" Our driver asked, trying his hardest not to get a tip.

Richter is a senior engineering student at Auburn I met through Jordan Ross, my travel companion from Spain and England. And while Tricia and I have joked about Richter being our adopted son, I'm only fourteen years older than him, so having someone mistake me for his father was a painful reminder of my rapidly graying hair.

The driver loaded our bags into the back of a black Mercedes and whisked us away to the hotel, a glass and marble monstrosity towering over the neighboring slums.

The next morning, I asked a man at the front desk if he could arrange a ten-minute ride on one of the auto rickshaws we'd seen on the roads. "Of course, Mr. Gibbs. You will follow me, please." We walked outside and he whistled for a rickshaw, and when it came near, the license plate said "CURRY" and it had Vishnu in the mirror. Okay, not really, but he did whistle for a rickshaw and appeared to scold the driver before motioning for me to take my seat.

As we left the hotel, my rickshaw driver attempted to cross eight lanes of traffic, and I immediately regretted ever asking to ride in what now I realized was a tiny casket on wheels. There were buses and trucks and cars and other rickshaws zooming in both directions, and we were about to partake in a live-action game of Frogger. And just before I asked my driver to let me out, he hit the gas, and I shut my eyes, and somehow we made it across to the next level. The rest of the ride was pleasant enough, except for the end, when the driver insisted I visit his friend's shop to see "all the fine merchandise; best prices in Mumbai, guaranteed."

■ ■ ■

I will not attempt to recount the history of India here, because it involves lots of dynasties with names I would likely misspell. However, I should note that from 1858 to 1947, India was ruled by the British Empire, and while there are many significant historical and cultural ramifications from this era, to me one of the most fascinating is that today there are nearly five times the number of English speakers in India as there are in the United Kingdom.

Christian missionaries have been visiting India ever since there have been Christian missionaries, and consequently there are almost as many Christians in India as there are in the United Kingdom, more than thirty-one million, according to a recent count. However, that thirty-one million makes up only about 2.3 percent of India's massive population.[2] Most of India, more than one billion people, practices Hinduism, and there is also a large Muslim minority with around 176 million adherents.

However, these numbers do not tell the full story. India is made up of twenty-eight states, and the percentage of Christians in these states varies widely. Mizoram and Nagaland, two small states in the northeast, have Christian populations near 90 percent. While Maharashtra, a state so crowded it would be the thirteenth largest country in the world were it to declare independence, has a Christian population of only 1 percent.

When I say Christian missionaries have been visiting India ever since there have been Christian missionaries, I'm talking about Thomas, he of doubting fame, who tradition says visited India in 52 AD. I learned this two weeks after this trip in the most bizarre fashion. When Auburn beat Alabama on a 109-yard return of a missed field goal to win the 2013 Iron Bowl, Tricia and I, in a mad fit of jubilation, crashed into the Indian family sitting below us. The next morning, we realized this family attends our church when we served them Communion. After the service, we introduced ourselves, and I spoke to the father, Suresh, about India.

Suresh said, "I was born in a state called Kerala, in the southern tip of India, and it probably has one of the highest percentages of Christians in the country. The reason we think there is this huge Christian population is because tradition has it that St. Thomas landed in Kerala, converted some of the leaders there to Christianity, and since then the

---

2. More than 1.2 billion people live in India, and people who make predictions about populations for a living predict India will pass China as the most populated country in the world in about a decade.

church has continued to grow. In fact I originally belonged to a church called the Mar Thoma Church, and we say our history dates back to 52 AD. We pride ourselves on this, and refer to ourselves as St. Thomas Christians."

"Was it difficult growing up Christian in India? Did you feel like an outcast or experience persecution?"

"No, India is very tolerant of all religions. Hinduism is, of course, the major religion, but you have Muslims, Sikhs, Christians, Parsees, and Buddhists. So there are all these religious groups living together, and the government has been very proactive since independence, instituting holidays for pretty much every religion. You'd wake up in the morning listening to the music that gets blared out from the temples, then the mosque would have their morning call to prayer, and we were used to all these things and didn't really think about it that much."

■ ■ ■

India is sort of shaped like an ice cream cone with one scoop on top, and Mumbai is on the west coast, near the top of the cone. We'd arranged a tour of the city through the hotel, and after lunch a driver and guide picked us up in another nice car. Vari, our guide for the day, asked how we were enjoying Mumbai as we pulled out into bumper-to-bumper traffic.

"We love it," Richter said, "but it's a little hot."

"This is the beginning of winter," she said.

"It's ninety-two degrees," I said. "You guys are going to have to come up with a better name for this than winter. Maybe call it second summer."

Vari laughed, and as we drove over the Mahim Bay on the Bandra-Worli Sea Link, Richter asked her what exactly we were supposed to call the city we were in.

"Not long ago the government changed the name from Bombay to Mumbai, because they said the name Bombay was an unwanted reminder of British rule."

"But you still call it Bombay?" I asked.

"Yes, Bombay, or sometimes Mumbai. I think in other parts of India if you say, 'I have been to Mumbai,' they will not know where you are talking about, but if you say, 'I have been to Bombay,' they will know. Many in India are resentful of the British, but the British brought us education, and they brought us infrastructure, and I for one am thankful for the British." Vari, for her part, sounded sincere, but I couldn't help wondering whether this was what she told all her English-speaking tourists. That said, Bombay really does roll off the tongue.

Our first stop that day was the Mahalaxmi Dhobi Ghat, an open-air laundromat that words are going to have a hard time describing. Workers, called dhobis, wash clothes and linens from local hotels and hospitals in concrete wash pens, each with its own flogging stone. The dhobis and clothes and pins seemed to go on forever, and even locals were standing on the bridge watching them work.

As we stood there, a train arrived at the Mahalaxmi station above the Dhobi Ghat, with passengers hanging out the doors on the side. I'd read about this before the trip and, probably like you, had seen it depicted in movies like *Slumdog Millionaire*, but to see it in person was something else. A man I'd met on my flight recommended avoiding local trains during rush hour because of something called superdense crush load, where fourteen to sixteen passengers are crammed into every square meter of floor space.[3]

I asked Vari about this and she said, "Yes, it can be very dangerous. People die on these trains every day in Mumbai. Many are pushed out of moving trains because of overcrowding, others are electrocuted while sitting on the roof, others are run over crossing the tracks, and sometimes people are simply crushed to death." People dying every day seemed like a bit of an exaggeration, but I did some reading that evening and, while statistics vary some, about ten people die on Mumbai trains every day.

"Would you like to see the train station where the final scene of *Slumdog Millionaire* was filmed?" Vari asked.

---

3. This would be a good time for you to put the book down, draw a square meter on your floor, and imagine fourteen people standing in it. Yikes!

"Yes," Richter and I replied in unison, and minutes later we were standing inside Chhatrapati Shivaji Terminus (CST), formerly known as Victoria Terminus, the busiest station in India. Outside, CST is impossibly ornate; inside it is impossibly crowded, so much so that Richter and I didn't have nearly enough room to demonstrate our Bollywood dance routine. Your loss, Mumbai.

■ ■ ■

Later that week, we flew from Mumbai to New Delhi on an Indian budget airline, and there were two interesting things from the booking process I'd like to note here.

1. Just before payment, I was asked to donate Rs 10 (about sixteen cents) to an organization called Save the Children. In return for this donation, I was promised "good karma."
2. Booking a flight from Mumbai to New Delhi on an Indian budget airline appears to be a great way to make sure your credit card company has your current contact information on file, because the minute I clicked submit, my phone rang. "Mr. Gibbs, this is Tyler from fraud protection services. We wanted to ask about a suspicious charge on your credit card." Funny thing is, I'm almost positive the call came from India.

On the flight, I sat next to a couple of Indian gastroenterologists on their way to a conference, and at one point, I mentioned visiting my mom and dad, and one of the guys said, "You still see your mother and father?"

"Yeah, quite often," I said.

"This is very good. We are pleased to hear this."

"Wait, do you know my parents?"

The man laughed and said, "No, I have just always heard that American families are not very close and am pleased to hear this is not always the case."

I later learned that many Indians live in joint households consisting of, for example, a mother and father, their male sons, their daughters-in-law, their unmarried daughters, and their grandchildren. I asked an Indian woman we met later in the trip what it was like living with her in-laws, and she took a deep breath before saying, "It is okay, some of the time."

On our descent into New Delhi, the city appeared to be engulfed by black storm clouds, but this turned out to be only smog. Before this trip, I occasionally checked the weather in India and was confused to see the forecast usually called for smoke, but once we landed, I realized smoke is an accurate description. According to some reports, New Delhi has even worse air pollution than Beijing, and we were visiting during a dry season, with no rain and wind to push the smog away. The only tradeoff for each breath filling your lungs with harmful carcinogens were the sunsets and sunrises, which shone quite lovely through the smog.

New Delhi was noticeably cooler than Mumbai, and after checking in at the hotel,[4] we requested a guide to show us around town.

"You would like to see New Delhi?"

"Sure," I said. "And maybe Old Delhi too."

"I think you will like to see New Delhi only."

The walled city of Old Delhi has been around since 1639, while New Delhi is just over one hundred years old. Consequently, the old city is dense and dilapidated, while the new city is more planned and structured. I had an odd feeling our hotel staff was trying to keep us from seeing Old Delhi, mostly because they kept telling us not to go to Old Delhi.

New Delhi was made the capital of India in 1931, and all branches of government are housed there. Our first stop was the Rashtrapati Bhavan, Indian's version of the White House, only, with 340 rooms under a massive dome reminiscent of the Pantheon in Rome, this sandstone home is four times larger than the big white one in Washington, D.C., and it has 100 percent more monkeys running around its lovely gardens.

From there we visited the India Gate, a 160-foot sandstone arch built to commemorate the seventy thousand Indian soldiers who perished

4. Our Delhi hotel was nice, but a little bizarre. Richter and I are almost positive there was a man on staff whose only job was to stand near the elevators and watch *Tom and Jerry* cartoons on a television built into the wall.

fighting with the British in World War I. Then we spent the rest of the day visiting a long list of famous Hindi, Muslim, and Sikh landmarks, including the Lotus Temple, Jama Masjid, Gurudwara Bangla Sahib, Qutub Minar, and Humayun's Tomb.

All of these things run together a little in my mind because each stop followed the same pattern. Our guide would tell us where to go once he parked, and the moment we stepped out of the car, a small crowd of men would gather round us, each of them offering to show us around the monument for a few rupees. The crowd would not disperse until you told each man individually you were not interested in hiring him as a tour guide, and sometimes they would still follow close behind, spouting facts of questionable authenticity. I began to think that on the Indian census, more than half the population list themselves as tour guides.

Traffic in New Delhi was about like you'd expect in a city where you can taste the smog, and the horn honking is loud and incessant, though Richter and I both noticed there seemed to be a language to it. There were short honks, long honks, double honks, and the like, and the closer you paid attention, the more you realized that each honk was saying something specific to the other drivers and pedestrians. That something was usually, "Get out of my way!"

We ate dinner at the hotel restaurant that evening. I had chicken curry with rice and chick peas and potatoes and some unleavened Indian bread stuffed with cheese called paneer naan, and it was all delicious and Indian and my stomach was no worse for the wear. You're pretty far into this book by now, so you're quite aware I'm no foodie. I ate at McDonald's in almost every country I visited. But after talking to several friends who'd visited India and contracted the dreaded Delhi belly, I vowed to be a little extra careful on this trip. So while my trip to India would make a terrible episode of Andrew Zimmern's *Bizarre Foods*, I made it through the week without experiencing a traumatic gastrological event. Besides, you didn't really want to read about my eating silkworm pupa anyway.

■ ■ ■

The next morning, we set out for the Taj Mahal in Agra, about a three-hour drive from Delhi on the Yamuna Expressway, a privately owned six-lane highway built by Indian billionaire Jaiprakash Gaur. On the way, our driver, Adesh, filled us in on his version of Taj Mahal history.

"Today you will see one of the Seven Wonders of the World. The Taj Mahal was built by Shah Jahan as a burial place for his third wife, his most beautiful wife, Mumtaz Mahal. It is said Jahan built the Taj Mahal because he loved his wife, but I do not believe this. I believe he only loved to sex her. She gave birth to fourteen children, and while birthing the last one, she die. So I believe Jahan felt guilty, because he sex her so much that she die, and in his guilt, he built the Taj Mahal." The rest of the drive, Adesh lamented the retirement of Sachin Tendulkar, India's most famous cricketer, who'd played his final match the day before, sending the entire country into a state of national mourning.

Even an hour outside of New Delhi, the Yamuna Expressway was smoky, and up ahead we'd occasionally see dozens of silhouetted figures dashing across the road. It was nice to get out in the countryside, to see a part of India besides the overpopulated cities, but even on the most desolate stretches of road, you'd still see people, just standing there, watching cars pass. There'd be nothing in sight but a small Hindu shrine and open fields, and yet there would be people, just milling about. I suppose in a country of 1.2 billion it's hard to find a place where there aren't people.

Before arriving in Agra, Richter and I both felt India hadn't quite lived up to the image of India we'd brought with us. And what I mean by that is we hadn't really seen any cows. But no sooner had we exited the expressway did we get a taste of the India we'd both imagined. There were herds of water buffalo wandering the streets, hundreds of cows in various stages of malnourishment tied to trees, horses pulling wagons, camels asking whether we knew what day it was, and monkeys, oh, the monkeys, I still have nightmares about the monkeys. We'd pass an abandoned building and notice a monkey or two loitering out front. But then on closer inspection you'd see monkeys on the roof and monkeys staring out from every window. Richter thought they were cute, but when I looked into their hollow eyes, I could just feel them thinking, "We will cut you."

Agra felt crowded in a way Mumbai and Delhi had not, despite the latter two ranking first and second on India's most populated cities list, while Agra, with only 1.58 million citizens,[5] is way down in twenty-third. In Agra we saw a family of seven or eight in the back of a rickshaw, the same size rickshaw I thought was a little cramped for one person. We saw more men than either of us could count piled into the back of a truck. And on the narrow roads through town, it felt like there was more foot traffic than vehicular traffic, and there was a lot of vehicular traffic.

We met Arti, our guide for the day, down the road a ways from the Taj Mahal, and the three of us took a rickshaw up to the gates. Within minutes we'd been approached half a dozen times by men wanting to be our guide for the day, and Arti would snap at them and they'd walk away sullen. By the end of the day, Richter and I both knew how to say, "They do not need a tour guide. Can you not see that I am their tour guide?" in Hindi.

In a courtyard outside the red sandstone walls that surround the Taj Mahal, Arti presented her version of the building's history, which, not surprisingly, did not mention Shah Jahan sexing his third wife to death. Then we walked through a massive arched gateway and for the first time saw the majestic mausoleum.

A couple of things about the Taj Mahal. First, it's massive. Sometimes through photographs or movies you are so familiar with a building before you actually see it that the real life version of it lets you down. That was not the case here. The Taj Mahal looked massive from a distance, and the closer you got, the bigger it became. Second, the closer you got, the more impossibly ornate it became. This is not the blank white building it sometimes appears to be in photographs.

---

5. If Agra were in the United States, it would be our fourth most populated city, behind only New York, Los Angeles, and Houston.

The entire structure is inlaid with colorful precious and semiprecious stones that sparkle in the morning sun.[6]

I was a little nervous about lunch in Agra, since we ate at a restaurant I hadn't previously vetted online to insure minimal likelihood of contracting stomach plague. On the door, a TripAdvisor decal assured me others had eaten here and lived, and inside, a man played sitar in the corner. A friendly waiter took our order and asked how spicy I would like my dish.

"Not very spicy," I said.

"And you?" he asked, turning to Richter Guest Gibbs.

"I want to try something really spicy," Richter said in a fit of insanity.

Our waiter actually laughed out loud and said, "Okay, we will cook yours with mild spice." Mild spice, it turns out, brought tears to Richter's eyes. If they'd actually served him something really spicy, I'm quite sure he would have died right there at the table.

Over lunch I told Arti a little about this book and asked if she knew any Christians in Agra. "I have many Christian friends and acquaintances," she said. "And being around them, I believe Christianity is a religion of love, peace, and forgiveness. In India it is a minority religion, but its significance is felt quite prominently because Christians often hold the key to a good education, as they administer many good schools and colleges. One doesn't go untouched by it."

I loved that line, "One doesn't go untouched by it." There are people much smarter than me debating whether Christians should attempt to spread the gospel by building schools or building wells or planting churches or preaching on the streets. But on a personal level, we should all try to live our lives so that those around us do not go untouched by the love of Christ.

■ ■ ■

6. Arti told us that Shah Jahan intended to build an identical mausoleum for himself across the river from the Taj Mahal, only his tomb was to be constructed from black marble. Sadly, for fans of identical ornate Indian tombs, Jahan was imprisoned by one of his sons and later buried next to his wife in the Taj Mahal.

On Sunday morning, Ramesh Landge, executive director of Cooperative Outreach of India, and his wife, Gloria, picked us up at our hotel and we attended one of the morning services at Delhi Bible Fellowship. I was feeling a little homesick, in part because I missed my wife and son, but if I'm being honest—and Zondervan has required that I be honest in this book—a large part of my homesickness had something to do with Auburn's miracle Hail Mary to beat Georgia the night before. A miracle Richter and I both missed because it happened long after midnight in India.[7]

Delhi Bible Fellowship's central worship center is located on a busy street (they're all busy streets) about a mile north of the president's estate. We entered the building on the second level, and there were dozens of worshipers sitting around a large opening in the floor where they could look down on the worship service below, the third of four worship services that weekend. There were seats saved for us in the overflowing room downstairs, and just as we walked in, the congregation began to sing "Because He Lives." And wouldn't you know it, as soon as we got to the line about how sweet it is to hold a newborn baby, all my homesickness swelled up in the form of tears and began falling from my eyes.

In many ways, writing this book made the world feel smaller to me. We live in a miraculous age, an age when in the length of time it takes to watch four movies, you can be on the other side of the planet. But it had been two weeks since I last saw my wife and six-month-old, and suddenly the planet felt enormous again. I'm not asking you to feel sorry for me here; I know people have to spend time away from family all the time. My brother-in-law Beau spent the first year of my nephew Garrett's life on tour of duty in Iraq, and in light of that, my homesickness does feel a little trivial. But missing home is part of travel, and on each trip, I'd have a moment or two when I regretted ever getting on a plane. However, that morning in India was the first time I ever missed home so much it physically hurt. No one around me seemed to notice

---

7. India is twelve and a half hours ahead of central standard time. That's right, twelve and a half. I think they added the half hour to make you feel even farther from home when you're there.

my tears, however, or if they did, they probably assumed I'd just had something spicy for breakfast.

■ ■ ■

We had lunch with Ramesh and Gloria after the service, and I asked about the religious culture in India.

"Indians have a deep-seated fear of God," Ramesh said. "People here are very religious and are searching for God, but they are searching for God in everything. And for that reason, they worship everything from trees to plants to animals."

"Are the Hindus you minister to receptive to the gospel?"

"Yes, because the caste system has dehumanized human beings, so, for instance, when we tell someone from a lower caste that they are created in the image of God, it resonates with them."

I don't think I'd ever thought of Hindus as particularly violent—all the hippy George Harrison Beatles songs seem pretty laid back—but India has seen its fair share of religious violence, between Hindus and Christians, Christians and Muslims, and Hindus and Muslims. While we ate, Ramesh shared stories about attacks on Christians by Hindu hardliners, and even told us of honor killings in some rural areas. India is the largest democracy in the world, and religious freedom is a fundamental right guaranteed to all Indians by their constitution, but Christians there still face persecution.

Ramesh continued, "Sometimes when someone converts, they are persecuted in a civilized way—they are deprived of their inheritance; they are deprived of seeing their family at gatherings. But other times, they are persecuted in the barbaric way. They are beaten and sometimes killed."

Lunch, as spicy as it was, sort of lost its flavor after hearing this.

■ ■ ■

"We should see Old Delhi," Richter said on our last day in India.

"I'm pretty sure they're not going to let us see Old Delhi," I said, "but we can ask."

"You do not want to see Old Delhi. You should see New Delhi," the concierge said with a smile after we'd asked for a tour of Old Delhi.

"We've already seen New Delhi," I said. "We'd like to see Old Delhi."

"New Delhi is very nice the second time," he countered, but we insisted, and he smiled and walked us outside and waved for a taxi, then he and the old Sikh driver exchanged some words in Hindi. "This man will drive you around New Delhi; just tell him when you would like to return."

"Old Delhi," I said.

"Okay, yes, Old Delhi."

So we hopped in and introduced ourselves to the driver, Partap, and he took us to see Old Delhi, which is, in a word, crowded.

Partap drove us to the Red Fort, then to Jama Masjid, a 350-year-old mosque, and at times the narrow roads were so densely packed with cars and people, I feared we would never move again. But sitting there among all that madness, I couldn't help but appreciate India. Yes, it is smoky, and yes, it is crowded, and yes, it doesn't always smell the way you'd like it to, but I loved every minute I spent there. The people we met were warm and friendly, and the country is at times so impossibly colorful and beautiful that I wish this book had photographs. Or better yet, I wish I could take you all there—hotel transfers are on me.

Of course, no tour would be complete without a requisite stop at a friend's souvenir shop, and as we stepped out of the taxi, mentally preparing ourselves to spend the next twenty minutes telling some guy we had no use for Kashmiri scarves, a man appeared out of nowhere and stuck a freaking cobra in my face.

"Agh!" I yelled, and jumped back in a very manly way. "Get that thing away from me."

The man with the cobra laughed, and Partap laughed, and I think the cobra laughed, so I lowered my voice a couple of octaves and said, "Seriously, get that thing away from me." Partap laughed again, but told the man with the snake to move along, and on second thought, I'm not sure I ever want to go back to India.

That evening as we pulled up to the hotel, I asked Partap how much we owed him for the day.

"You should just pay me what you like, and I will let you know if it is the right amount."

I try to be sensitive to other cultures. I really do. But why some people insist on turning the simplest of transactions into a game show I will never understand. "Partap, we have no frame of reference here; just tell us what we owe you and we will gladly pay it."

"I could not, sir."

So I lied and said I needed to go to the room to get my billfold and instead told the man at the front desk, "Remember the guy you hired to take us to Old Delhi?"

"New Delhi?"

"No, Old Delhi, but that doesn't matter. He won't tell us how much money we owe him for the tour."

"Where all did you go?"

I told him, and he said, "Pay him two thousand rupees." So I walked outside and handed Partap two thousand rupees, which he counted slowly, before looking at me with a shrug. Then he got in his taxi and drove away.

"Was it enough?" Richter asked when I walked back inside.

"I think so," I said, though I'm pretty sure Partap was upset we just gave him the correct amount instead of figuring it out with him through trial and error. And looking back, I see how rude it was to resist participating in the culture that I was visiting. So I vowed the next time someone wanted to barter, I would play along, but I didn't have another opportunity in India. An hour later, the hotel transferred us to the airport, and two long flights later, we were back in Auburn, where the air is clean and the cobras are few.[8]

---

8. I wanted to mention here that my friend Jordan Green was supposed to travel with me to India in November 2012; however, he forgot to apply for his visa and I had to cancel the trip at the last moment. It's a shame, too, because we were going to see Guns N' Roses in Mumbai. So we tried again in November 2013, but the day Jordan received his visa in the mail, his wife, Mindy, had surgery because her cancer had returned. Mindy passed away one month later, and she is missed dearly by all who knew her. This chapter is dedicated to Mindy's memory and, I suppose, to Jordan's forgetfulness.

TURKEY

Istanbul was Constantinople
Now it's Istanbul, not Constantinople
Been a long time gone, Constantinople
Now it's Turkish delight, on a moonlit night
—Jimmy Kennedy, "Istanbul (Not Constantinople)"

The music had changed. Before, it had been fun and just a little too loud to talk over. But now it was pulsating, building, and as a man with flowing white robes and a tall red hat approached the stage, I felt something dramatic was in store.

"Who is that?" I asked Esref, the first Muslim I recall ever having dinner with.

"That man," Esref said, "is a Whirling Dervish."

The Dervish did not look like a happy man. He scowled out from the stage onto the sea of diners now filming him with their phones. Then he began to whirl and whirl and whirl. He whirled for five minutes, worshiping in what has to be the most dizzying way possible.

"You will notice," Esref said, leaning over to me, "his right hand is open and turned toward the heavens to receive God's goodness, while his left hand is facing the earth."

The Whirling Dervish finally stopped whirling, to a smattering of applause, and, to my surprise, walked off stage without wobbling noticeably. I reached down and took a drag off the apple-flavored hookah pipe Esref had ordered for our table, and as I coughed out the smoke, I said to Esref, "This has undoubtedly been the most interesting dinner of my life."

Esref smiled and said, "I'm glad you are enjoying Turkey."

■ ■ ■

Justin Zoradi, my friend from Portland and founder of These Numbers Have Faces,[1] and I arrived at Istanbul Ataturk Airport that morning running on fumes. We'd used our eighteen-hour stopover in London as an excuse to see our favorite soccer club, Manchester City, play Tottenham Hotspur at White Hart Lane, and though we enjoyed the 5-1 win immensely, we both regretted not finding some time in the previous thirty-six hours to sleep.

---

1. Right now, These Numbers Have Faces is educating and empowering college students in South Africa, Uganda, and Rwanda in the hope of raising up a new generation of leaders committed to the growth and development of Africa. Please check them out at *www.these numbers.org*.

At the arrivals gate, we approached a young man holding a sign with my name on it, and he walked us outside, where we waited on the van to drive us to our hotel. "Where are you from?" he asked us, and we told him the United States.

"I am Russian," he said, "but we can still be friends, no?"

"Sure," Justin said.

"Here are my top five states," our new friend continued. "New York, California, Florida, Chicago, and Los Angeles."

"Those are good ones," I said. "I'm from Alabama, and Justin is from Oregon."

"Yes, Alabama and Oregon," he said. "These I will add to my list of favorites."

Our hotel was located in the Sultanahmet, the old city of Istanbul, named after Sultan Ahmet I, ruler of the Ottoman Empire from 1603 to 1617. We checked in and walked up to the rooftop for a stunning panoramic view of the city. Domed mosques with tall minarets dotted the low skyline, and across the Bosphorus Strait, the Galata Tower rose high above the rest of the city. It was the kind of view you could look at for hours—or a few seconds, since it was January and freezing.

That evening we had dinner with Esref, a friend of some friends in Auburn and a native Turk. Esref picked us up at the hotel, then tried to navigate the winding roads of the Sultanahmet, without much luck. He'd only recently returned from living in Spain for the past seven years, and some one-way roads were now flowing in opposite directions, while other shortcuts had disappeared. At one point we may have been driving on the sidewalk, but remarkably we ended up parking right next to the restaurant, in the shadow of the famous Blue Mosque.

Esref ordered plate after plate of delightful Turkish food, which is not to be confused with Turkish delight, a gummy dessert that, at least for me, doesn't quite live up to its moniker. Over chicken, lamb, and rice, among other things, we talked to Esref about the amount of fear some of our friends had expressed about our visiting Turkey.

"I think I was told to be careful more times before this trip than any other."

"I was told to pretend to be Canadian," Justin added.

"Speaking of fear," Esref said, pulling out his phone, "this man's website was emailed to me. Do you know him?"

I took his phone and began scrolling through the website of perhaps the most hate-filled individual on the internet, and if you are familiar with the internet, you know that's saying something. This guy, whose name I'd rather not mention because you'd be tempted to google him, was directing most of his hate toward Muslims and President Obama, which to him, of course, were one and the same, and the dozens of people commenting on his posts were regurgitating the hate, only with worse grammar and spelling.

"No," I said, handing Esref his phone back, "I've never heard of him, but he sounds a little crazy."

"Here is my email to this man," Esref said, handing me his phone again so I could read the text of a heartfelt message he'd composed, which I doubt the recipient ever read. Esref's letter made me sad because I know he has American friends who love him dearly and pray for him and try in every way they know to show him the love of Christ. Perhaps it's no easier for me to reconcile that Esref and some radical fundamentalist are both Muslim than it is for him to reconcile that this angry man on the internet and I both claim to be Christian.

"There is a lot of money to be made by scaring people," I said. "If a website scares you, you will keep going back and reading it, because eventually not reading it becomes even scarier than reading it. You're not going to change this guy's opinion of Muslims, because his livelihood is built around demonizing Muslims. If Muslims aren't scary, this guy is unemployed. Our hanging out, having dinner, and discussing faith doesn't really fit his narrative, you know? If his next blog post is titled, 'I Had Dinner with a Very Nice Muslim Man,' not many people are going to click on it."

I heard the words coming out of my mouth but knew I was guilty myself. Not of fearmongering, or any kind of mongering for that matter, but of simply being fearful. I said in the beginning of this book that Christ did not call us to a life of fear, yet I know my blood pressure rises when I notice a couple of bearded Arab men boarding my flight. And sadly, I believe American Christian culture has bought into the fear-sales idea just as much or more than the secular culture. Take a stroll through your local Christian bookstore and check out the prophecy section. Half the books will have atomic-bomb mushroom clouds on the cover. And then go over to current events, where you will find books with titles like *JIHAD AMERICA: The Coming War with Islam That Will Likely Claim the Lives of Your Children and Take Away the NFL.*

We tried to pay for dinner, but Esref insisted on treating us, and as he dropped us off at our hotel, he said, "Tomorrow is Jumu'ah, Friday prayer. I think it would be very interesting for you to visit a mosque. You can sit in the back and observe the service."

"Sure," I said, "that sounds like a great idea." And by great idea I meant it sounded like the worst idea I'd ever heard. I could just see the headlines on CNN: "American in Istanbul Labeled Infidel, Detained for Entering Mosque during Friday Prayer." I found out later in the week we could have done this without any problem. It's a shame too, because I could have met Muslim men, I could have shared with them the thoughts behind this book and my reason for being in Istanbul. It could have been a truly unique experience, and I missed it out of fear. I pray to be less fearful the next time.

■ ■ ■

The next morning, Ugur, a self-described secularist and another friend of a friend, met us at our hotel and spent the day showing us around the Sultanahmet. As you may recall from history class, Istanbul was once the capital of the Eastern Roman Empire, also known as the Byzantine Empire. Back then the city was called Constantinople, after the Roman emperor Constantine, who rebuilt the city and made it his capital in 330 AD. And while the Western Roman Empire fell in 476 AD, the Eastern part went on for nearly one thousand years more, until Constantinople fell to the Ottoman Turks in 1453.

Our first stop was the Topkapi Palace,[2] where those conquering Ottoman sultans lived for nearly four hundred years. And as we toured the massive residence, Ugur said, "When a new sultan ascended the throne, he would have all of his brothers and half-brothers ritually killed to prevent one of them from later staging a coup."

"So you'd rather your brother not become sultan," I said.

"No, and some of the sultans had many brothers. Mehmed III had nineteen brothers killed when he became sultan."

"Wow," Justin said. "So they were just beheaded?"

"Actually they were strangled with a silk cord, so as not to shed royal blood. Later this practice was done away with, and the sultan's brothers were simply confined to a room their entire lives, until the sultan died and one of them became the new sultan. Of course, spending your entire life locked in a room isn't ideal, and some of these men were already mentally unstable by the time they were called upon to reign."

From the palace, we made our way to Hagia Sophia, a former Eastern Orthodox basilica built in 537 AD. I say former because when the Turks conquered Constantinople, Mehmed II converted the building into a mosque. It remained a mosque until 1935, when the newly formed Republic of Turkey reopened the great building as a museum.

Hagia Sophia is massive. For nearly one thousand years, it was the largest church in the world, and inside, elements of Christianity and Islam reside side by side. There are breathtaking mosaics of Jesus, Mary, and assorted saints, along with gigantic medallions hanging in each corner of the room bearing the name of Muhammad and his successors, called caliphs.

"You'll notice the church faces Jerusalem," Ugur said. "However, Muslims pray facing Mecca, which is to the southeast of Istanbul. That is why some elements in the church, like the Mihrab, are askew from the rest of the building."

The Sultan Ahmed Mosque, also known as the Blue Mosque, sits

---

2. One of the museums at the Topkapi Palace contains the staff Moses used to part the Red Sea, along with a lock of Muhammad's beard, although Ugur said with a laugh, "I am not convinced of the authenticity of these items."

directly across from Hagia Sophia, but it was closed for Friday prayer when we walked over. So instead, we had lunch next door, and the call to prayer echoed through the cold winter day as we placed our order.

"Most people I know have never heard the call to prayer," I said to Ugur. "I'll be honest, it's a little scary sounding to Western ears."

"It's not that scary," Ugur said. "He's basically saying, 'God is great. There is no God but God. Hurry to the mosque for prayer.'"

"That's it?"

"Pretty much, except the first one, the one that has probably been waking you up each morning, they add the line, 'Prayer is better than sleep.'"

Outside the second-story window of the restaurant, we could see men placing their prayer mats on the sidewalk because inside the mosque was too crowded. And over lamb and rice, I watched them bow, kneel, and rise while reciting their prayers.

"There aren't many mosques in Alabama," I said.

"Yes, I have been there." Turns out Ugur went to college in Oregon and had been to all fifty states while working for a Turkish carpet business in America.

"A few years ago," I told him, "Muslims tried to build a mosque in Tennessee, but it didn't go well. I think some local politician went on television and told everyone this was the first step toward sharia law. We all get a little freaked out about sharia law."

"Building a mosque is one thing," Ugur said, "but I do not believe everyone should have to listen to the call to prayer five times a day. It is very loud, and not everyone wants to hear it."

"Maybe they could send out text messages."

Ugur laughed. "Yes, the text to prayer could work."

After lunch we were able to visit the Blue Mosque, and I must say, it's one of the most beautifully ornate buildings I've ever been inside. It was completed in 1616, and it's the blue tiles inside that give the mosque its moniker. We entered, shoes in hand and mouths agape as we stared up into the magnificent dome 141 feet above our heads.

Ugur said, "Outside you may have noticed six minarets. This was a contentious issue when the mosque was built, because four minarets was the maximum, and only Masjid al-Haram, the Grand Mosque in Mecca, had six. But a seventh minaret was added to the Grand Mosque and the issue was resolved."

Velvet ropes kept the throngs of tourists contained in the back of the mosque, and up front you could see Muslim men and boys continuing to pray, while other Muslim men were taking photographs of themselves. It was an odd mix of worship and tourism, and it reminded me a little of the service we attended at the Metropolitan Cathedral in Rio de Janeiro. We took some photos too before walking outside to put our shoes back on.

■ ■ ■

I'd met Ugur through my friend Murat, a native Turk who's lived in Washington state for the last twenty years. Murat became a Christian in 1998, and as Justin and I walked back though the Sultanahmet, I recalled asking Murat before the trip if his conversion had strained his relationship with his parents.

"My family is a little bit more modern," Murat told me. "They were never involved in religion too much. My family respects me and I respect them, and they will always want the best for me, so there was never a problem in my life over what I wanted to believe. Actually it was good, because before I became a Christian, I was a little more troubled, and by that I mean going out too much and too much drinking, and when I became a Christian and dropped those things, my family was happy."

Murat continued, "For Muslims, Jesus is a prophet that they know, so it wasn't a big shock. Of course, when you begin to explain the doctrines, it becomes a stretch for them to understand. But I understand these things because of the work the Holy Spirit is doing in my life, and when you try to explain Christianity to someone who isn't a Christian, it can be difficult for them to understand. So no, my family has always been very supportive of me, but for many others, growing up in strict Muslim homes, it can be very difficult."

I asked Murat about some of the positives and negatives he saw in Christian culture, and he spoke warmly of the sincere love he's always felt in the church, but added, "A problem is when you tell someone you are a Christian, they ask what kind. What are your beliefs? Are you Protestant, Catholic, Baptist, nondenominational, are you this or this or this? In the Muslim faith, there isn't as much of this. You go to any mosque and it's pretty much the same: you pray five times, you listen to a priest, and you leave. With Christianity, it's almost like, 'I'm better than you because you don't believe the way you are supposed to.' People look at it almost like a contest and will tell you that their knowledge and relationship with God is the true way. Because of this, Muslims will often say, 'Your Bible has changed.' They see all the translations, the King James, the Message, and they tell you the Quran hasn't changed. This part of Christianity can be very difficult to explain to the Muslim people."

■ ■ ■

A couple of days later, Justin and I flew south from Istanbul down to Izmir, a city of four million on the Mediterranean coast. The domestic terminal was insane that morning, and Justin and I joked about how personal space differs from culture to culture. In Turkey I got the feeling if you weren't spooning the next person in line, others would assume you weren't actually in line and would attempt to wedge themselves in front of you.

From the window of the plane, I could see all of Istanbul sparkling in the morning sunshine, and I said to Justin, "I think there's a mosque on every street corner down there." It sort of made me think of Alabama, where there's a church with a steeple on every corner, and it reminded me of something Ugur had said earlier in the week. "In terms of daily life," he said, "Turkey and the United States are almost identical, except for one is called Christian and the other Muslim. In Turkey the coastlines are more liberal, and inland is more conservative, a lot like the States. And for many here, being a Muslim doesn't actually mean observing the rules; it's more part of the culture than something to live by. But no matter how religious a person is or isn't, holidays are celebrated by everyone here, just like in America."

Around 99 percent of Turks are registered as Muslims, and as if to drive this point home, our flight had personal televisions featuring the Quran, alongside Western and Turkish movies. And while there are only around 120,000 Christians in Turkey today, it wasn't always that way. In fact Turkey has perhaps the richest Christian history of any country not named Israel. Paul was born in Turkey, and so was Timothy. Those seven churches John sent his revelations—all in Turkey. The Nicene Creed was written in Turkey, the followers of Jesus were first called Christians in Turkey, at Antioch,[3] and the New Testament books of Galatians, Ephesians, and Colossians were all letters written to Christian communities in modern day Turkey.

We were flying to Izmir for a tour of Ephesus, the ancient Greek city where Paul spent three years, and at the airport we met Zeynep, our guide for the day. On the forty-five minute ride to the ruins, Zeynep talked about life in Turkey.

"Most people in Turkey are Muslim," she said, "but Turkey is a very moderate country. You can do what you like here. Some women cover their heads; I do not. Some people do not drink alcohol, because the Quran forbids it, but I sometimes drink with my friends and family. Here you are free to do what you like."

Our first stop that day was the House of the Virgin Mary, a restored house and shrine on Mt. Koressos, about four miles from the ruins of Ephesus. Tradition says the apostle John brought Mary to Ephesus after Jesus' crucifixion; however, this house wasn't discovered until 1881, when a French priest began searching for it based on the visions of a German nun in a rather confusing story that I had trouble following.

My ears were popping as we kept winding our way up Mt. Koressos, and as we pulled into the parking lot, Zeynep said, "This is a sacred place for Christians, but also for Muslims, because Mary is the only woman mentioned in the Quran. I get very emotional when I visit this place." Then she added, "Oh, and make sure not to take photographs

3. The same Antioch of Holy Hand Grenade fame.

inside the house. There are policemen in plain clothes who will confiscate your camera and not return it."

After touring the house, we drove back down the mountain, passing a massive golden statue of the Virgin Mary, then parked at the upper gate to the ancient city of Ephesus. Justin and I thought the ruins you could see from the road were all there was to see of the city, but we were wrong. The city keeps going and going, down a long narrow path lined with marble columns in various stages of ruin. You walk by the Temple of Hadrian, past the beautiful terrace houses with unbelievable mosaic floors, before turning right in front of the breathtaking Library of Celsus, and near the lower gate, you visit the massive theater, where a riot began after Paul's missionary work started to affect the pocketbooks of local silversmiths who specialized in silver statues of the goddess Artemis.[4] No silversmiths were rioting this day, though there was a small Japanese boy singing loudly and earning the applause of those of us resting in the theater.

After Ephesus we had lunch at a carpet shop run by the Turkish government. Handmade Turkish carpets are world-renowned, and the government educates local women while paying them a salary in the hope that the tradition of handmade carpets will not be lost in the age of machines. And because everyone here is on a salary, the salesmen were not nearly as pushy as the ones we'd met in the Grand Bazaar. However, they did put on quite a show, unrolling carpets and covering a large showroom with wool, cotton, and silk rugs.

"How much is this one?" I asked, pointing to the large silk rug that would look great in our den back home.

"This one will be thirty thousand," he said.

"Lira?" I asked.

"Euro," he said.

Needless to say, the forty-thousand-dollar carpet did not go home with me that day.

At this point, we'd finished our tour and still had about six hours

---

4. We visited the Temple of Artemis later that day. One of the Seven Wonders of the Ancient World, all that's left of it today is a single column, while the rest of the ruins are on display at the British Museum in London, naturally.

left before our flight back to Istanbul, so Zeynep asked, "Would you like to see my hometown?" We said sure, and we drove fifteen minutes to Kusadasi, a resort town on the Aegean Sea.

Kusadasi was beyond beautiful. We sat up on a hillside looking down on the town and harbor, while Zeynep filled us in on the absurdly affordable local real estate market.

"Why don't we live here?" I asked Justin.

"I don't know."

Zeynep was getting married in the coming months, and the carpet shop had let her take two carpets to see which one she thought would look best in her new home. "This does not typically happen on tours," she said, "but would you mind if we drove by my parents' house to drop off these carpets?"

We said of course not, and soon Zeynep's mother was inviting us up for Turkish coffee and chocolate. Her mother did not speak English, but she could not have been a nicer host, and we all sat around the living room laughing as Zeynep's slightly insane dog jumped from couch to couch.

When Tricia and I travel, she likes to plan one thing a day and leave the rest of our time open for happy accidents. This goes against my nature, because I read tour books and panic if I don't see everything there is to see in a place. But so many of my favorite moments from this book were not planned, like having coffee in the home of a delightful Turkish woman in Kusadasi.

"You are very lucky my father is not home," Zeynep told us as we were getting ready to leave. "Since I am not married, it is forbidden for men to come inside our home. If he were here, he would be required to kill you both." She must have seen the panicked glances Justin and I exchanged, because she laughed loudly and said, "I am just kidding. My father is a very moderate man."

Zeynep took us, slightly shaken, back to the airport where, tired of chicken and rice, we had McNuggets from a McDonald's that I believe dates back to the early Byzantine era. Then we boarded our flight back to Istanbul.

■ ■ ■

On Sunday morning, we took a taxi to Nations Church, an interdenominational church in northern Istanbul. We followed directions sent from Kim and Ed, Americans living in Istanbul I'd met through my friend Shawn Smucker, and we passed through a Sunday morning street market before finding the office building with the church's sign out front.

Inside, we were offered coffee and tea and met dozens of wonderful people who all informed us that Kim and Ed had been in a car accident on their way to church that morning. They were okay, but they would be late.

Worship that morning consisted of praise songs led by a woman on keyboards, another woman singing, a guy playing guitar, and another guy playing some sort of cool drum that he sat on. We sang songs in English, then switched to Turkish, then switched back to English, and later Justin said, "I like going to a church like this; it gives me an us-against-the-world feeling."

I knew what he meant. Christianity feels different when you're in the minority. The sixty or seventy of us up on the fifth floor of that office building shared a special bond. Yes, it's the same bond we share with believers back home, but something you don't really notice when you live in a place with Christian book kiosks at most gas stations. And as if to drive home this point, during the sermon on Jesus' temptation in the desert, which was given in English and translated into Turkish, the Islamic call to prayer echoed loudly through the open windows.

Kim and Ed slipped in near the end of the service, and afterward the four of us took the metro to a nearby mall for lunch. "How do cheeseburgers sound?" Ed said. "We figured you guys might be tired of chicken and rice by now." Justin and I wanted to hug him.

Over lunch, I asked about the difficulties Turkish Muslims face when converting to Christianity.

"Here Islam is seen as a part of someone's Turkishness. Being Muslim and being Turkish are almost one and the same, so a convert would be seen as losing their Turkishness in some sense. Converts are sometimes called Greeks or Armenians, two nationalities Turks associate with Christianity. We saw similar things in central Asia, where Muslim converts were referred to as 'becoming Russian.'"

"Are there other parts of Turkish, or even Muslim, culture that make it difficult to share the gospel?" I asked.

"Back in the States, we often fall into the trap of attaching right behavior to salvation, and as a result there are many people who think good behavior will get them into heaven. This isn't an accurate presentation of the gospel, but it makes even less sense here. Muslims already know they shouldn't lie, cheat, steal, drink, commit adultery, and so on. And because they are driven by outward behavior over inward change, many times they follow the rules better than we do. Not to say they are perfect, but overall, they have as much a veneer of morality as we do."

"So the 'look at all this sin in your life; you need Jesus' approach doesn't really fly here?"

"No, because you're just addressing the symptoms of sin, but the sin nature has not changed at all. The truth is that the good news of Jesus Christ has a lot to do with Christ becoming Lord of all creation and our submitting our lives to his lordship."

I think most of us would be fearful of living as Christians in a country where Muslims make up 99 percent of the population, maybe even consider hiding our faith, but Kim told us, "When you come here from the West, Turks expect you to be Christian." So hiding your faith is out of the question, because Turks are going to assume you're a Christian anyway, and as for fear, Kim and Ed told us Turkey was home, and when they spoke of their neighborhood and the terrific relationships they have with their Muslim neighbors, there wasn't the first hint of fear.

I told them I thought fear keeps many people from experiencing wonderful places like this, and Kim said, "We visited Iran not long ago; it was honestly one of the best family vacations we've ever had."

I realize that is probably the strangest sentence you've ever read, but after hearing them talk about their trip, I was ready to go.

Of course, life isn't as easy for Turkish Muslims who convert to

Christianity. Besides others no longer considering you a Turk, Kim and Ed told us many are disowned by their families, and some are beaten, tortured, or even killed.

"It's funny," Justin said on the metro ride back to the hotel, "we're so quick to quote verses about your losing your family or being hated for Christ's sake, but those verses are a lot easier to quote in America."

"Yeah," I said, "the concept of being hated by your parents for following Christ isn't easy to grasp when your parents are the ones who introduced you to Christ."

■ ■ ■

Our last evening in Turkey, we went to see Galatasaray, the most famous soccer club in Turkey,[5] then spent some time walking around Taksim Square before going back to the hotel and looking out on the city one last time from our hotel's roof. Then we slept about an hour before the obscenely early alarm rang, and a taxi drove us to the airport. Justin and I had different flights home—he was flying through Manchester; I was routed through Paris—so we said goodbye to each other, and then I said goodbye to Turkey, but not before adding it to the ever-growing list of places I hope to see again one day.

---

5. I spoke a lot about fear in this chapter, and I must admit I was a little nervous about going to see Galatasaray, so I asked our hotel manager if we'd be okay at the match. "Mr. Gibbs," he said, "wherever you travel in life, there can be danger." This was not reassuring, but nevertheless we had an incredible time.

EPILOGUE

Once you have traveled, the voyage never ends, but is played out over and over again in the quietest chambers. The mind can never break off from the journey.

—Pat Conroy, *The Prince of Tides*

Here we are, at the end of the book, where I'm supposed to wrap up everything with a bow and tell you the things I've learned from exploring Christian culture around the world, but I'm afraid this may prove difficult. You know how your elevated heart rate continues to burn calories for minutes after you've stopped exercising? Yeah, me neither, but I've read about it, and my travels for this book have sort of been like that.

As we get older, the years seem to pass more rapidly, in part because all of our days are more or less the same and we remember them as a long boring blur. Travel is a break in that blur. It's a touchstone that you will look back on months later, years later, decades later, because it stands out so in your memory. And as you reflect on your travels through different seasons of your life, you will continue to learn new things.

So I will try to tell you what I've learned from experiencing Christian culture around the world, but it's a little like asking a guy what marriage has taught him immediately after kissing his bride. I know what I learned from these trips in the short term, but what they will be teaching me years from now, I can only imagine.

■ ■ ■

Over the last two years, I spent time with Christians in countries I've always considered the enemy of America, Christianity, and football with helmets. This had an immediate impact on my worldview, because all of a sudden an Arab Palestinian is calling me brother, and a Chinese woman is wishing me happy birthday, and a Russian man is telling me how precious my son is. These days when I wake up and check Facebook and Twitter, I feel like I need to consult Rosetta Stone to decipher all the foreign languages, and I love it.

The gospel of Luke tells us the story of a religious leader asking Jesus what he must do to inherit eternal life. When Jesus confirms the answer is to "love the Lord your God with all your heart and with all your soul and with all your strength and with all your mind, and to love your neighbor as yourself," the religious leader asks Jesus, "Who is my neighbor?"

No one ever asks Jesus, "Who is my enemy?" We think we know who our enemies are. They are people with political views different from ours. And people with religious views different from ours. And sometimes they are even people who adhere to branches of Christianity different from ours.

But when this religious leader asked Jesus who his neighbor was, Jesus turned the question on its head by telling the parable of the good Samaritan, a shocking tale of a beaten Jewish traveler being rescued by a hated Samaritan.

I don't think of myself as a bigoted person, but we all have our blind spots. Mark Twain famously wrote, "Travel is fatal to prejudice, bigotry, and narrowmindedness, and many of our people need it sorely on these accounts. Broad, wholesome, charitable views of men and things cannot be acquired by vegetating in one little corner of the earth all one's lifetime." Well, traveling the world, encountering Christian cultures other than my own, brought the parable of the good Samaritan to life. I began to see perceived enemies as neighbors and watched as prejudices, some I didn't even know I had, slowly melted away.

■ ■ ■

God and country became a running theme on my travels. I met many believers who found the patriotism they see in the American Church a little disturbing. And not to say these people are not patriotic themselves; if you saw some of them screaming during a World Cup match, it might scare you to death. However, they do not believe a Sunday service is the best time to praise their country. Later, when I walked under the red flag of the People's Republic of China to enter a church or when we prayed for God to save the Queen of England, it did feel rather strange, though certainly no stranger than it would feel for a foreigner to stumble into the Fourth of July service at any number of Bible Belt churches.

If you want a glimpse of how this feels without traveling across the world, go to your local Christian bookstore and find the God and country section, where they sell T-shirts, paintings, and other trinkets that pair the American flag with Jesus, the cross, or a verse from Scripture. Now try to imagine those items with a Russian flag or a Chinese flag or a flag from any other country. Kind of weird, huh?

Americans are also quick to associate our very imperfect nation with our perfect God, without stopping to consider the consequences of such an association. Because of this, throughout the world there are people who assume anyone they meet from America is a Christian. A man in Turkey told me, "Most of the Muslims I know think Christian women are very loose, because American and European women come here on the cruise ships and sleep with Turkish men." This is just one example of what can happen when you make an entire nation ambassadors for Christ. And don't forget the places I visited where a certain religion was just seen as part of the culture, like Muslims in Turkey or Catholics in Italy. If we keep referring to America as a Christian nation, don't we run the risk of lost people assuming salvation is based on their birth certificate?

Please don't get me wrong. I'm not saying you shouldn't be proud to be an American[1] any more than I'm saying you shouldn't be proud of your children or your alma mater. Heck, I tear up more often than not during "The Star-Spangled Banner," and who doesn't cry when

1. Where at least you know you're free.

Rocky knocks out Ivan Drago? I've been to a lot of countries now, and I'm more appreciative than ever that God placed me here in the United States. But there is a line out there between patriotism and idol worship, and as I experienced Christianity around the world, I began to see that line more clearly.

■ ■ ■

There are somewhere around 2.2 billion Christians on our planet, and if you are an American Christian reading this book, odds are most don't agree with you on a number of things. I was raised in a Southern Baptist church and moved to a United Methodist church a few years ago, and before traveling, I believed the bulk of Christendom consists of those two churches, along with the Presbyterians down the street, whom we both usually beat to lunch.

These three groups make up around 28.6 million people, which sounds like a lot, until you consider that more people live in Tokyo. And until you consider it's less than half the Assemblies of God adherents worldwide, or less than half the Ethiopian Orthodox adherents worldwide, or less than one-fifth the Russian Orthodox worldwide, or less than one thirty-ninth the Roman Catholics worldwide.

I realize that ours is a large and old faith, and meeting Christians from different denominations around the world helped me appreciate this. Because I fear I'd fallen into the trap of thinking that heaven will be full mostly of American Christians, while all these other denominations around the world will miss the boat because they've been doing it wrong. I know the arrogance that leads to thoughts like that is off the scale, but like I said earlier in the book, it's always nice to be reminded that we are not experts on the things we know nothing about.

I remember a few weeks after visiting Russia, I was complaining about the songs we were singing at my home church, then I immediately remembered the Orthodox Christians I'd met, who view worship as work, not as a Sunday morning concert that requires my critique.

When you travel, you will meet believers who worship in different ways, who express their faith in different ways, who interpret certain

Scripture passages a little, or a lot, differently than you do. And you might find yourself somewhere like the Church of the Nativity in Bethlehem, singing hymns in a cave with pilgrims from around the world. And you might stop and think, This is weird; I have some important doctrinal disagreements with a lot of these people. But then you'll remember you've all come to this cave in the West Bank to worship the same Savior. That Savior is a great place to start the conversation when you meet Christians from different backgrounds and heritages. You'll learn something about them, and they just might learn something about you. Misconceptions will fade on both sides, and this often-dysfunctional global family we belong to will become a little less dysfunctional.

■ ■ ■

Speaking of dysfunctional, every year on the Friday following Thanksgiving, hordes of shoppers trample little old ladies in an attempt to secure bargain-priced plasma televisions, among other things. And every year, Christians call foul, not that little old ladies have been trampled in a shocking display of materialism gone mad but that the stores refuse to associate the name of Christ with their little old lady trampling sales, going instead with something more generic like Holiday Sale.

I say this because if I think I'm facing persecution in America, in a place everyone refers to as the Bible Belt, then it's a slap in the face to my brothers and sisters in Christ around the world who are living with real-deal, life-or-death persecution.

Look, I'm not saying it's easy to be a Christian here. The things we are called to do as believers—love our enemies, don't judge, forgive one another, don't worry, be humble—none of it is easy. It's not easy in Alabama and it's not easy in North Korea. But if we believe living the Christian life is difficult in America because of persecution, then I think we're being just a touch overdramatic. Have you ever been tortured by the police because of your beliefs? Yeah, me neither, because the police go to my church.

It was eye-opening to go to places where Christianity isn't the norm, where in your entire school you might be the only person who confesses Christ, where conversion could cost you your standing in society or your family or your life. Don't you find it interesting that while we fear persecution, home church pastors in China fear the end of persecution, because they know comfort and complacency will take its place?

Because that's our challenge, finding the urgency to live out our faith in a part of the world where it's hard to sense the need for urgency. I know comfort sounds a lot less scary than persecution, but when we're talking about things that keep us from living the life Christ has called us to live, they're all scary. We're not always the best at diagnosing our own problems, but spending time with Christians in other cultures, and even Americans living overseas, really helped me identify the biggest stumbling blocks to my faith, and the War on Christmas isn't one of them.

■ ■ ■

Minority Christianity isn't easy and it isn't comfortable, and sometimes it isn't even safe, but it is beautiful. When we left the small church service in Istanbul, my friend Justin said, "Those people are truly doing life together. Everyone knows everyone and they are on a common mission. You don't get that much anymore in an American megachurch." I felt this throughout my travels, visiting small congregations in places like Japan and India. I said earlier that I've always thought of minority Christianity as struggling Christianity, even failing Christianity. But traveling the world, I began to understand that just because a country doesn't have Bible Belt numbers doesn't mean that we cannot learn something from the believers there or that God isn't at work, doing mighty things through that faithful minority.

Back home, bigger is better, and while there is nothing wrong with large churches, I'm afraid they do sometimes cause us to miss the little things that can bring so much meaning to the Christian life. After experiencing minority Christian culture, I truly began to understand the importance of small groups and Sunday school classes back home, because a thousand-member church will always struggle to feel like community. People can attend large church services for weeks and months and years and not know a soul, and this cannot be right.

We like to dream big in America, even in the church, and that's fine. We have the numbers and resources to do big things for Christ. But traveling the world, I learned we need to dream small as well. I learned that doing life in a close, supportive Christian community is essential, even if that community is only a small group inside a much larger body of believers. I believe this will be a focus of mine for years to come, because when you see a close, supportive small group of Christians intently focused on loving God and loving their neighbors, you see a beautiful glimpse of the kingdom of heaven.

■ ■ ■

I thought about these things on my flight from Istanbul to Paris, pausing briefly to look out the window of the plane as the rising sun reflected brightly off the Eiffel Tower. And I've thought about them a lot since that last long trans-Atlantic flight back to Atlanta.

And while standing in line for immigration, I began leafing through the passport I've had for less than four years. It'll need more pages soon; there are only one or two blank ones in the back. The rest are full of stamps and visas, each one a reminder of something—a bike ride through the snow, a walk along a rocky shore, a worship service in a language I don't speak, a delicious meal in the home of new friends. And handing my passport to the officer, I realized it was over. This crazy adventure I'd set out on more than two years ago had finally come to an end.

The officer stamped my passport, stamped my arrivals card, then handed them back to me and said, "Welcome home, Mr. Gibbs."

And walking through the Atlanta airport after my last trip, I still did it. I took a peek at the departures sign. Buenos Aires, Cape Town, Seoul, Oslo—there are still so many places I plan to see. But my wings are clipped for a little while. It's your turn to go explore God's creation.

Bon voyage, y'all.

ACKNOWLEDGMENTS

In the acknowledgments of my previous books, I've attempted to thank every living person I know, in the hope that every living person I know would in turn purchase my book, because who wouldn't buy a book with their name in it, right? However, the problem with acknowledging everyone I know is that apparently I do not know everyone that I know, and even after thanking hundreds of people, most of whom had nothing to do with the creation of my books, I inevitably left out a second cousin or a high school friend, then spent the better part of the next year feeling bad about it. So for this book, I've decided to keep things short and simple and assume no one really reads the acknowledgments anyway.

I want to thank Tricia, for letting me go and for being there when I came home.

I want to thank Kim and Alan Gibbs and Karen and Harrell Day, Mimi and Paw Paw and Mia and Granddaddy, respectively, for helping Tricia with Linus while I was on the other side of the world.

I do not want to thank Linus, because leaving home is the only requirement of a travel book, and he made leaving home very difficult.

I want to thank my editor, Carolyn McCready, and you should thank her too, because you didn't have to read my first draft.

I want to thank my agent, Chip MacGregor, in part for selling my books and doing all the other things an agent does, but mostly because I feel important when I can drop the phrase "my agent" into casual conversation.

I want to thank Caleb McNary and Jess Buttram for reading early drafts of this book. In return I let them choose what font their name would appear in. **Caleb** went with Helvetica; **Jess** chose Rockwell.

I want to thank Chris Davis Jr. one hundred and nine times.

I want to thank Becky Philpott, Londa Alderink, Bridget Klein, Brian Phipps, Mark Bast, and everyone at Zondervan.

I want to thank Rusty Hutson, Brian Johnson, Josh Agerton, Pat Bethea, Lee Cadden, Lynn Blount, and the rest of our church family at Cornerstone Church in Auburn.

Finally I want to thank my travel companions for saying yes when I called and asked if they wanted to go to India or China or Turkey. I want to thank everyone who suggested something to see or someone to meet in each country I visited. And of course, I want to thank all the locals and expats I met in person or spoke to over Skype or even interviewed via email. I cannot thank you all enough, because this book would not exist without your help.

And I should probably stop here, but I feel like I should thank my nieces and nephews, Garrett, Morgan, Ava, Jake, and Chandler. They didn't really help with this book, but they'd probably like to see their names in print. However, if I thank them, I'll want to thank their parents, Ashleigh and Beau and Lori and Johnny, and if I do that, I'll still be typing names six pages from now. So I'll just have to stop typing and trust that no one really reads these anyway. Except for you, you who read every word of the acknowledgments. You know who you are, and I want to thank you too.

A Call to Travel

I wish you'd been there. I wish you'd been there on Sugarloaf, looking out across Rio at Christ the Redeemer. I wish you'd been there in Jerusalem, walking in the footsteps of Jesus. I wish you'd been there in Maastrich, so you could have told me not to try the herring. And now that it's over, I want to encourage you to go and see some of it for yourself.

It's not easy. I know that. I asked my social network, a lovable bunch of quiz takers and essential-oils salesmen, what keeps them from traveling and seeing the world. Some said fear, with one citing the movie *Taken*. But far and away, the two things mentioned most were time and money.

In regard to money, I know the words *cheap* and *international travel* are rarely used in the same sentence. Susan Heller said, "When preparing to travel, lay out all your clothes and all your money. Then take half the clothes and twice the money." She's totally right about the clothes, but trust me, there are cheap ways to travel, and I don't mean flying on cargo planes full of cattle and sleeping on hostel floors.

In the opening chapter of this book, I mentioned paying for all my flights with frequent flier miles. I was able to do this by travel hacking, an admittedly bizarre method that involves signing up for multiple travel credit cards and racking up hundreds of thousands of frequent flier miles. These miles come in the form of sign-up bonuses ranging from forty thousand to a hundred thousand miles, and they are usually earned after spending a certain amount in the first three months. We'd spend the required amount and earn these bonuses by paying bills and buying groceries with our cards, and then we'd always pay off our balances in full each month. If you are debt free, on top of your finances, and not planning to purchase a house anytime soon, it can be quite lucrative. If you're in debt, your finances are a mess, or you're about to buy a home, just forget I mentioned it.

Tricia is a doctor, so I won't pretend that we are poor, but we certainly didn't have enough cash in the bank to pay for twelve international trips. But I knew if I could pay for the flights with frequent flier miles, and if I could pay for a friend's flight with frequent flier miles, and if that friend would split hotel costs with me, I could do it all for around fifteen thousand dollars, which I suspected would be the amount of my book advance if I could find a publisher. And in the end I was right. Using 1.8 million frequent flier miles, I was able to book forty-two flights for $8,847 in taxes, airline fees, and the occasional credit card annual fee. These forty-two flights would have cost a little over ninety-three thousand dollars if I'd paid for them with cash. Split hotels, trains, tours, museum entrance fees, airport parking, and taxis cost $7,246, for a grand total of $16,093, which was a little over budget, but I do still have 1.2 million frequent flier miles, so I'm not complaining. And in the spirit of full disclosure, I should mention that most of our trip to Uganda is not included in the final number, since it was a missions trip and our payment to our church was a fully tax-exempt donation. My in-country expenses in Italy are also not included, because once we got there, my parents insisted on paying for everything. And finally, I did not include meals in the grand total, since I would have had to eat every day even if I'd stayed home.

Sure, you may have to scrimp and save and plan the trip a couple of years in advance, but I wouldn't have written this book if I didn't think the sacrifice wasn't worth it. And if you commit about the same amount of time it took reading this book to learning about the different travel hacks out there (not all involving credit cards, don't worry), you can save yourself thousands of dollars. I'll show you where to get started on my website, *www.chadgibbs.com/travel.*

As for time, yeah, I can't really help you there. Most gainfully employed parents can't take a dozen trips outside the country just to experience Christian cultures other than their own. I'd encourage you all to become Christian humor travel writers, but I don't really want the competition. But hey, even if you can't go overseas, remember we live in a large and diverse country. Maybe skip the beach or Disney World one year and take the family on some rambling road trip you'll remember the rest of your lives. That said, if your kids hate it, don't tell them it was my idea.

I fear the best I can do is hope to catch you while you are young. If you're in high school or college reading this book, you are likely in a much better position to go and see the world than if you're middle-aged with kids. Besides, if you're going to make memories that last a lifetime, you should make them while you're young, otherwise you're not getting your money's worth. So study abroad. Take a gap year before college. Take one after college. Teach English in China. Teach Chinese in England. Just go, and don't forget to send me a postcard.

Still not convinced? Okay, let me try to articulate what I see as the benefits of traveling. Travel breaks us out of our routine. Do you know why the years seem to pass more quickly as we get older? It's because we stop experiencing new things. As kids we experienced new things daily, and consequently it felt like twelve years passed between our birthday and Christmas. But when each day becomes identical, we remember them in a long indistinguishable blur. Travel is many things, but it is rarely boring, and while it won't make you live longer, it will make it feel like you do.

"But there are scary things out there. I don't want to die!"

I suppose there are scary things out there, but there are scary things everywhere. Next time you are on the interstate, glance over at the car next to you, and as you watch the driver attempt to eat a chicken wing while texting a photo of said chicken wing to a friend, ask yourself how safe you feel. The United States has a low murder rate; you are probably not going to be murdered here. But 102 countries have lower murder rates, and you are even less likely to be murdered there. In fact, you probably won't be murdered in any of the 103 countries with higher murder rates than the United States either.[1]

As for fear of flying, I get it, I truly do. Tricia will be happy to recount the terrified look that didn't leave my face for the duration of our thirty-minute flight from Birmingham to Atlanta on our honeymoon. But if I can get on a plane, you can too. And hey, you don't have to fly anywhere just yet. We live in an amazing country. A country where you can drive for six hours and all of a sudden people stop putting sugar in their tea and start pronouncing their *r*'s. Take a road trip like we did, but remember that can be dangerous too; there are people texting pictures of chicken wings out there.

In all seriousness, Christ didn't call us to a life of fear, and fear shouldn't keep you from traveling. Yes, it's easy to sit at home because you've been told there are people out there who hate you, but it's far more rewarding to go meet those people and realize they don't. Remember what Mark Twain said about travel's effect on prejudice, bigotry, and narrowmindedness, because as those three things fade, so does a lot of fear.

God has filled the earth with a lot of wonderful people, and meeting them is one of the great rewards of travel. Sometimes the conversations will be lighthearted and you'll talk about sports or Beyonce. But sometimes things will go deeper and you'll talk about faith. Their questions will challenge you, their answers will challenge you, and if you believe you've got this whole Christianity thing figured out and there's nothing left to learn, you may be troubled by the whole experience. But if we discuss these things only with friends who share our opinions, drive the same minivan, and live in the same white-picket-fence suburb as we do, we are missing out on a large part of the conversation.

---

1. I visited a lot of countries for this book, but do you know which country I visited has the highest murder rate? The Bahamas.

Speaking of that white picket fence and minivan, a lot of the people you'll meet out there don't have those things. In fact more than half the people in the world live each day on less than I spend at Starbucks every morning. When you travel, you will meet people who live in poverty, you will meet people affected by the slave trade, you will meet families torn apart by war, and you will experience compassion in a whole new way. How your compassion will manifest itself, I do not know, but I do know this: many missionaries and nonprofit founders and all-around awesome people were inspired to change the world after going out and seeing the world. Traveling the world, experiencing Christian cultures other than my own, has changed me for the better, and I'm excited to see how it will continue to change me in the years to come. But not only that, I'm just as excited for you to see the world, to see how your experiences will change you and how you in turn will change the world.

But consider this fair warning: traveling does not get traveling out of your system; it only makes you want to travel more.

I'll see you on the road.

God and Football

Faith and Fanaticism in the SEC

Chad Gibbs

Where Faith, Football, and Fanaticism Collide

Renowned humorist and die-hard football fan Chad Gibbs knows he cannot serve two masters, but at times his faith is overwhelmed by his fanaticism. He is not alone. This year, more than six million people will attend an SEC football game. They'll spend thousands on season tickets, donate millions to athletic departments, and—for three months a year—they'll order their entire lives around the schedule of their favorite team.

Gibbs and his six million friends do not live in a spiritually void land where such borderline idol worship would normally be accepted. They live in the American South, where according to the 2008 American Religious Identification Survey, 84 percent indentify themselves as Christian.

This apparent contradiction Gibbs sees in his own life, and in millions of others', led him on a journey to each of the twelve SEC schools to spend a game-day weekend with rabid Christian fans of various ages and denominations.

The result… *God and Football*, an illuminating, laugh-out-loud look at the place where faith, football, and fanaticism meet.

Available in stores and online!